Praise

Unfinished Business

"*Unfinished Business* is a prescriptive, compassionate, user-friendly guidebook for the heart, infused with hard-won wisdom and true concern for the emotional health and authentic well-being of us all. Both science-based and deeply personal, the work in this book helps us to understand our challenging life events from an entirely different perspective and offers us an invitation to lovingly face ourselves, our fears, and our heartbreaks, so we can finally heal from the past and move on. By using her own difficult losses and past traumas Melanie encourages us to organize our complicated histories and take inventory of what was lost so we can enthusiastically grab hold of all that is yet to come. It's an eye-opener. I loved every page."

—CINDY CRAWFORD, International SuperModel,
Entrepreneur, TV Personality, *New York Times*
best-selling author, Mom

"In *Unfinished Business*, Melanie Smith explores the powerful force that can hold us back from fulfilling our potential for success, health, and happiness. The accessible, evidence-based steps in this book can help us put our unfinished business behind us so that we can become the best version of ourselves and flourish. Beautifully written and a necessary read in these disorienting times."

—TAL BEN-SHAHAR, *New York Times* best-selling
author of *Happier, Being Happy* and creator of the
most popular course in Harvard University's history

"Honestly taken aback by the process Melanie so eloquently writes the reader through. Her ability to help us understand our emotional history as well as how to set it free is a kind of superpower for those of us determined to heal and reach our greatest potential. Engaging. Insightful and a life changer for me. Grateful to have read it! It's that good."

–ERIC YAVEBAUM, *New York Times* best-selling author of 7 books including *Leadership Secrets of the World's Most Successful CEOs*

"*Unfinished Business* is a beautifully written survival guide for anyone with a past, a present and a future. An inspiring roadmap for those of us who have ever had doubts about our place in the world. I've used it myself and found it phenomenally helpful. This one is a must read!"

–DR. BEVERLY KAYE, *Wall Street Journal* best-selling author of *Love Em or Lose Em, Up is Not the Only Way, Hello, Goodbye*, and *Help Them Grow or Watch Them Go*

"*Unfinished Business* is a clarion call to liberation found through the sacred portal of the heart. Discover how embracing your grief opens the door to all aspects of being: the soul, the energy body, the physical body, and the conscious and unconscious mind. Complete with personal stories and potent exercises, this is a book that our world needs desperately in order to heal from the trauma and loss that eventually visit us all. A work of profound compassion."

–ANODEA JUDITH, Ph.D., best-selling author of *Eastern Body, Western Mind; Wheels of life, Charge and the Energy Body*, and *The Global Heart Awakens*

"Throughout our thirty-plus-year friendship, Melanie's constant desire has been to help people heal and live authentically. *Unfinished Business* distills all of her knowledge, tools, and wisdom into a practical, step by step guide that is a must-have resource to help us all navigate our painful pasts and ever-changing, complex lives. From the very first page you know that you are in amazing hands as you learn, grow, and heal from Melanie's hard-earned strength, compassion, honesty, and insights. This book is a true work of heart."

–NANCY MCKEON, Actress, Writer, Producer, Director, Mom

"*Unfinished Business* is a tour de force, both practical and big-hearted. Smith shows us a new way to think about loss, heartbreak, and trauma. Through her process of untangling and organizing our painful histories and clearing the emotional clutter that blocks the view into our deepest selves, she helps us imagine how our lives would be transformed by meeting every obstacle with questions like, 'How will this strengthen me for a better?' and 'What's possible when I take full responsibility for my life?' Truly original and essential work for us all!"

–MARILEE ADAMS, PH.D. best-selling author of *Change Your Questions, Change Your Life*, CEO of The Inquiry Institute

"Melanie Smith's *Unfinished Business* is required reading for anyone feeling stuck in the past or in unhealthy patterns, yet instinctively knows that there is so much more they are capable of becoming. Most people are unaware of the deep pain of their past, and how it is holding them back. Many more have resigned themselves to their suffering, and think it is permanent and impossible to ever be "finished." But *Unfinished Business* provides hope, tools, and skills that create lasting change and healing once and for all. If you are looking to transform your relationships, professional life, and most importantly, yourself, Melanie's scientifically supported and proven work changes you on a cellular and energetic level so that you can live fully, abundantly, joyfully and claim the life you knew deep down was possible all along."

–MARY CURRAN HACKETT, best-selling author of *Proof of Heaven* and *Proof of Angels*

"Throughout this book you will find pieces of yourself in Melanie's words and wisdom. Every page exudes compassion for each of us struggling to find unerring meaning in our heartache. She brings us into her world so we can connect deeply with our own and takes us on a journey that is not only life changing but also heart-opening. It is revolutionary in its perspective on our painful and often traumatizing pasts. By the end you will find yourself releasing tears of gratitude and fully embracing your boldest dreams of the future. This book is transformational and truly enlightening."

–LEANNE JACOBS, best-selling author of *Beautiful Money*, wealth expert and leadership mentor

Unfinished Business

Unfinished Business

8 Steps to Heal Your Trauma,
Transcend Your Past,
and Transform Your Life

Melanie Smith

SHE WRITES PRESS

Published 2023
Printed in the United States of America
Print ISBN: 978-1-64742-515-9
E-ISBN: 978-1-64742-516-6
Library of Congress Control Number: 2023906714

For information, address:
She Writes Press
1569 Solano Ave #546
Berkeley, CA 94707

Interior Design by Tabitha Lahr
Chart on page 16: JuliyaS © vectorstock.com

She Writes Press is a division of SparkPoint Studio, LLC.

Company and/or product names that are trade names, logos, trademarks, and/or registered trademarks of third parties are the property of their respective owners and are used in this book for purposes of identification and information only under the Fair Use Doctrine.

All identifying information, names, and details of clients and students have been changed to protect the confidentiality of my clients. However, even as I have respected their anonymity, I have remained true to the essence of each of their stories.

For more information about this book, my services, and these practices, please visit www.workwithmelaniesmith.com.

To Marge and Monroe, my mother and father.
For the many traumas you endured, and for the
love you gave despite it all.

For Gideon, my son. You are the meaning
behind everything.
I carry your heart. I carry it in my heart.

Contents

Introduction xix

❋ **PART I**

Chapter 1: My Personal Journey 1
    The First Whisper • 3
    Finding the Rainbow • 5
    The Life You Were Meant to Live • 8

Chapter 2: Unfinished Business 11
    Breaking the Loop • 14
    What Is Unfinished Business? • 15

Chapter 3: Under the Unfinished 22
    Unfinished Business Is Universal • 24
    What Is Grief and How Is It Connected to UFB? • 25
    Not All Grief Is the Same, but
        It All Matters the Same • 25
    How the Unfinished Business Program
        Is Different • 30

Chapter 4: Understanding the Whole 32
    Soul • 34
    The Conscious Mind • 36
    The Unconscious Mind • 37
    The Three Brains Theory: How Our Body
        Communicates • 39
    Bioenergetics • 41
    The Soma • 42
    Bringing It All Together • 43

Chapter 5: Program Overview 46
  What to Expect • 49
  Things to Keep in Mind • 51

❀ PART II

Chapter 6: Rethink 55
  Prework: Tilling the Soil • 58
  Homework Follow-Up • 63
  Higher Self-Talk • 63

Chapter 7: Lesson 1 65
  Why We Are the Way We Are • 67
  Models, Mantras, and Beliefs • 68
  Lesson 1 Homework: Identifying Your Models,
    Mantras, and Beliefs • 74
  Homework Follow-Up • 78
  Higher Self-Talk • 78

Chapter 8: Lesson 2 80
  The AACTs of Life • 82
  Where Our AACTs Come From • 84
  Belonging and Shame • 86
  Lesson 2 Homework: Naming Our AACTs and
    Taking Responsibility • 91
  Critical Notes Before You Do Your Homework
    for This Chapter • 101
  Homework Follow-Up • 102
  Higher Self-Talk • 103

Chapter 9: Lesson 3 105
  What Is Charge? • 109
  What Is Incomplete Charge? • 110
  How Charge Shows Up • 113
  Why Charge Matters • 114
  Charge Changers vs. Charge Choices • 117
  How Charge Starts Getting Blocked • 119
  The Hunt for Charge Changers • 121
  Short-Term Gains, Long-Term Losses • 123
  Overcharged vs. Undercharged • 125
  Common Charge Changers • 126
  Taking Total Responsibility: Revisited • 132
  Lesson 3 Homework: Understanding and
    Diagnosing Charge • 133
  Tips for How to Process Charge • 140
  Moving into Charge Choices • 141
  Homework Follow-Up • 142
  Higher Self-Talk • 123

Chapter 10: Lesson 4 144
  Acute vs. Chronic Trauma • 147
  Putting Words to Feelings • 154
  The Four Rs • 157
  Lesson 4 Homework: Completing the
    Puzzle of You • 159
  Homework Follow-Up • 170
  Higher Self-Talk • 171

❋ **PART III**
Chapter 11: Recap 175

Chapter 12: Lesson 5 177
  Who Is Taking Up the Most Room? • 179
  Gone but Not Forgotten • 182

Complete or Repeat • 183
Lesson 5 Homework: Taking Responsibility
   and Letting Go • 184
Homework Follow-Up • 195
Higher Self-Talk • 196

Chapter 13: Lesson 6 197
Recharge to Discharge • 200
Saying Goodbye • 202
Lesson 6 Homework: Release Through Writing • 203
Homework Follow-Up • 207
Higher Self-Talk • 209

Chapter 14: Lesson 7 210
The Happier Ending • 212
Lesson 7 Homework: Your Happier Ending • 215
Homework Follow-Up • 221
Higher Self-Talk • 223

Chapter 15: Conclusion 225

APPENDIX 1: Holmes and Rahe Stress Scale 229
APPENDIX 2: Stress Indicators Continued. 234
APPENDIX 3: Identifying *Your* Heartbreak
   Category and Type. 236
APPENDIX 4: Terms Overview. 238

Endnotes 243
Acknowledgments 246
About the Author. 253

I no longer look at heartbreak through
the eyes of the wounded.
Each loss, every change, all transitions
are now a trail of gems,
polished stones on the path toward my highest potential.
They are sacred reminders of my purpose,
my wisdom, and my promise to carry them forward as a
gift for others.
My resilience and courage are the map;
each difficult negotiation, the terrain.
Now, there is nothing I cannot recover from.
There are only things I have yet to uncover and understand,
disguised as good-byes
I have not been willing to say.

—MELANIE SMITH, 2018

Introduction

Have you ever wondered . . .
Who you would be if *nothing bad had ever happened to you*?

If you'd never lost anyone or anything; if you'd never seen any dream shattered?

If no one had ever made you feel like you were not enough? Taught you limitations? Told you who you could or couldn't be?

If no one had ever broken your heart, betrayed your trust, or done any of the thousands of big and small things we humans do—to one another and to ourselves?

Who would you be if you got to say everything you've ever left unsaid?

If you could put your past in the past and truly forgive yourself and others?

How would you show up in the world?

What would be different about your relationships?

If you are single, how would you date differently?

If you are partnered, how would the bond between the two of you change?

What kind of people would be in your life? Who would no longer be in your life?

Would you still have the same job? Would you spend your free time the same way?

Would the biggest and scariest things you dream about be closer or farther away?

Who would you be if you could finally complete the incomplete and find fresh, solid ground again?

As if the past had never happened at all?

....

Questions like these started entering my mind when I was around twenty-eight years old, just after I made the difficult decision to leave my job starring on the long-running, much-beloved *As the World Turns* and move from New York to Los Angeles. I was reeling from the recent loss of my mother to a rare form of cancer that had started with a simple stomachache. I was desperately searching for a soft place to land and make sense of what was to come next. Years had passed since I'd left my small town of Scranton, Pennsylvania, to make my way in the Big Apple and prove to myself I had what it took to succeed in this world. Throughout that time, I had pushed the stress of life and the incomplete emotional residue of my challenging early years—including a life-threatening childhood illness—deep down inside me. Now, however, that residue was beginning to percolate and rise to the surface.

These questions, and others like them, continued to occupy my thoughts for years to come while I continued to pursue my career as an actor in LA. They rose in volume as I became more established than I had ever dreamed possible. They grew even louder after the tragic death of my sister, and louder still after I made the decision to leave my television career of nearly three decades once and for all and move back East to raise my beautiful son. And after divorcing my son's father, losing my dream home, selling my business, and suffering a financial restructuring that hit me so hard it nearly unmoored me—they became positively deafening.

These questions were the catalyst for my passionate search to understand what it is that happens to us on the way to our most powerful lives—what it is that interrupts our potential and stops us moving on our rails at the speed we were built for.

They are, in fact, the heart and soul of this book.

What these questions represent is a deep curiosity about why we know so little about ourselves and who we are becoming while we're on our way to becoming it. This curiosity is the driving force that inspired my return to education in the fields of grief, trauma, psychology, philosophy, coaching, bioenergetics, and alternative healing modalities, and my decision to go deep within myself through the practices of meditation and yoga. All of these things—external studying, internal reflection, and deep work on myself—have informed the creation of this book and the journey we are about to embark on together.

Throughout the years, one question in particular has always led the pack and stayed with me morning, noon, and night: *Who would I be, could I be, if nothing or no one had ever gotten in my way?*

Chances are, you bought this book because your life isn't what you had planned or hoped for. Or maybe it is, but even so you don't feel happy or fulfilled. You can't get out of your own way; you keep repeating old patterns. You feel, perhaps, like your life is one endless loop of dissatisfaction and frustration. Or maybe you've recently experienced a loss, and your heart is hurting.

Even if your loss happened a long time ago, I'm guessing there is one loss—or there are many—you suffered at some point that you can't seem to recover from. Or, perhaps, you feel bitter from past situations where you never got to fully express yourself or get closure. Maybe it's that you've carried the weight of heartbreak your whole life without quite being able to put your finger on why, and you long to see what living with a free heart and spirit feels like. You may find yourself asking the same question I asked myself so many years ago: *Who would I, could I, be if no one or nothing had stepped into the trajectory of my potential— and is it too late to make it right?*

Well, rest assured that the process you're about to participate in will be transformational.

The first goal of this process is to help you identify unresolved hurts, stories, patterns, beliefs, and relationships, as well as the pain caused by heartbreaks, deep disappointments, unwanted changes, and transitions. The second is to help you complete the incomplete and release the past. The third is to aid you in the continued release of the unfinished business in your life—all those uninvestigated falsehoods you have "bought into" and continue to use as silent road maps on your journey—so you can install a new and clear GPS that will guide you to the places in life you've always dreamed of. In the weeks and months to come, you will resolve your unfinished business so you can heal your trauma, transcend your past, get to know yourself more deeply, and create and claim your destiny!

What are your dream results? Do you want to heal your heart, trust again, love again, or have peace of mind and soul? Do you want to experience breakthroughs in your business, career, family dynamics, health, or mental and emotional well-being? Perhaps you want to experience greater passion or an even deeper love in your life. Maybe you long for more authentic connections to yourself and others.

Each one of us has our own vision of what would constitute a deeply fulfilling and meaningful life, but what stands in the way of those dreams is very similar, if not the same, for most of us: the unfinished business of our past.

Here's the good news: you are not alone on this journey, and by the end of this process you will see that every loss, every change, every transition is a trail of gems that can lead you down the path to your highest potential. There is nothing you can't recover from; there are only things that you have yet to uncover and understand.

How do I know? Because this work has not only changed my life, it has also changed the lives of the hundreds of clients and students I've worked with globally over the years. The process I'll share in the chapters to come is profoundly life-altering, heart-opening, and time-tested. I can tell you firsthand, after following the steps laid out in this book, I no longer look at heartbreak and trauma through the eyes of the wounded. Instead, I see it through the eyes of a compassionate, open-hearted traveler living a life of passion, fulfillment, and authenticity.

By the time you've finished this book, you will too.

Why I Wrote *Unfinished Business*

People often ask me why I spend my life trafficking in the arena of loss, change, transition, heartbreak, trauma, and, well, simply put, all areas of unfinished business.

My answer is threefold.

First, like all of you, I have been through a lot of loss and heartbreak in my life. Second, I have been graced with the ability to face and heal my wounds, which has allowed me to—through hard work—go deep enough to find ways through the difficult pain and disappointment life can expose us to (and let me tell you, life has certainly challenged my tenacity, resilience, and determination, all of which are required to make it in our world). Finally, it's because I knew it was impossible for me to create the life that was *truly* meant for me when I wasn't certain who I *truly* was.

Most of us are completely unaware of what's holding us back—what's keeping us from growing into who we *would* be, who we *could* be. The most insidious things in our lives are the things we don't see at all. They are the things of the past we've buried or hidden, or are even completely unaware of. Think of your life as a garden: you can see the flowers or the weeds that reach up from the earth, but you likely very rarely think about what's going on beneath the surface.

> *"This might sound simple, but I cannot overstate this: The single most important thing is recognizing what the problem is in the first place."*
> —Nadine Burke Harris

All those things you blindly tolerate? All those incomplete relationships, losses, beliefs, identities, and stories that either nourish or starve your decisions, actions, feelings, and choices? They are controlling your behavior in the world. They are the reasons why you sometimes feel stuck, stunted, lost, or even trapped.

It is what we cannot see that creates the *who* we present to the world—and at its worst, it can make you feel so overwhelmed by it all that you feel like you're being buried. This is what makes deep work so complicated. But as you move through this book, you will find that it can be a lot easier than you might imagine, as long as you have the right tools.

I have always wanted to ascertain that all the loss I have suffered in my life has served a greater purpose—that I faced those trials not simply so *I* could learn how to live or to grow my soul but also so I could help *others* to "out" the sneaky principles on which many of us have been raised, primed, and even force-fed. This work came from my profound desire to find out *who I could be* if I fully healed myself of past traumas and freed myself to claim my deepest desires.

My life hurt me. My family hurt me. The world hurt me. I hurt myself.

Then I fixed it.

I worked hard to calm and eventually clear the undercurrents of past beliefs and identities that had pulled my life in a direction at cross-purposes to the one I should be following—the one in which I was inexhaustibly determined to go—for far too long. And then I figured out how to help other people do the same.

I lay myself out here as a sort of alchemical laboratory you can engage with rather than a centerpiece you feel forced to look at. I wrote this as a heart hack to get you back on track—back to the life you were made for, the life you were meant to live.

What You'll Find in This Book

This book delineates the process I have developed over nearly two decades as a tool for recovery, forgiveness, and healing. It is basically a holistic system for unearthing, clearing, and closing the unfinished and very dangerous business of our lives—for not just plugging but *eliminating* those leaky places that steal our souls and rob us of our most necessary and profound energy.

And that starts with investigating all the things going on beneath the surface.

To explain how this works, let's go back to our garden metaphor:

Just like weeds that grow and crowd out a healthy garden, our old, unresolved issues can fill our system with underground interference and stop us from thriving. In order to grow to our greatest possible heights, we must dig deep into the garden of our life—of our soul—and pull out all the roots and tendrils that are strangling our potential. We must get to the unfinished business of the past. Until we do, no amount of external work will fix the problem; as a matter of fact, thinking that it will is one of the false beliefs that got us into trouble in the first place.

Think of it this way: If you have a massive weed problem and you ignore it, regardless of how much water and sunlight you lavish on your flowerbed, the weeds will eventually take over—swallowing up your healthy plants and choking them to death. Over time, left unchecked, the weeds win. *The weeds always win!*

The same goes for you. Unless you get to the deep root of your issues, no matter how much effort you put in, no matter how many books or affirmations you throw at the problem, you're still going to end up feeling stuck, miserable, misaligned, and crowded out of your own life and dreams.

> *"When I let go of what I am,*
> *I become what I might be."*
> **–LAO TZU**

The work you will do in this book will help you to get to the root of all the subtle weeds, hidden just underneath the surface of your life, that are destroying more possibilities than you can imagine. In our work together, we're going to get to those roots, yank them up into the light, clear the soil, and replant so that you can flourish and grow into the highest and best version of yourself.

But before we really dig into all this, let's start at the beginning—with my own story, and the core philosophies that lie at the heart of *Unfinished Business.*

Part I

Chapter 1:
My Personal Journey

Being born into challenging conditions will turn a person into an inner explorer and seeker.

I was born a seriously ill infant. I underwent major surgery when I was just eleven months old, after which I was left in the hospital alone (the circumstances were beyond my parents' control—they had five other children to take care of) until I recovered well enough to come home. I was in and out of the hospital for eleven years after that . . . and so went my entrance into the world.

When you are a sick kid, people treat you differently. They see you differently. A sense of belonging never really gets baked into you. There is a feeling of being on the outside even when people invite you to join them on the inside. A space exists between you and others, and that space persists no matter how deeply you long to be close to them.

There is a modern variation on something Italian Dominican theologian St. Thomas Aquinas once said that goes, "For those who understand, no explanation is needed. For those who do not understand, no explanation is possible." This was the haunting sentiment of my childhood. And the more heartbreak and hardship I experienced as the years went on, the more this underlying sense of solitude pervaded my being.

"The greatest damage done by neglect, trauma, or emotional loss is not the immediate pain they inflict but the long-term distortions they induce in the way a developing child will continue to interpret the world and her situation in it."

–GABOR MATÉ

I watched my mother have her first stroke when I was five years old. It was shocking, overwhelming, impossible for me to process or absorb. As my father and older sister carried her up the stairs like a rag doll, I buried my head back in my coloring books, intent on forgetting all I'd just seen.

Six years later, at eleven years old, I witnessed my mother in crisis once again—this time lying beside my bed, covered in blood. This was her second stroke, and her first and only cardiac arrest. I had to get her to the emergency room by myself.

There are few traumas that go as deep as that of a child desperately trying to save their mother's life. I wouldn't understand this fully until many years later, when I finally realized that this was the reason the same abject terror I'd felt at eleven would frequently arise in me in stressful (but far less dire) situations.

Aside from my mother's erratic health, I also had a very difficult relationship with one of my sisters. I loved her very much, but she repeatedly broke my heart and trust with tricks, teasing, and physical outbursts that would leave me bruised and vulnerable. Back in those days, it was looked upon by the adults around us as nothing more than "kids' play that got out of hand"—but the wounds her actions inflicted on me went deep.

I have always believed that when a child suffers a great trauma early in their life, a crack opens in the universe and connects them to a deeper part of their being, turning them inward and creating an insatiable seeker. This was certainly the case for me. The impactful events and challenges I experienced in my early years led me to spend a lot of time alone throughout my youth—writing, creating, and trying to know my own soul.

To be clear, I was neither neglected nor abused by my parents; in fact, I was a very loved child. I did well in school; I was praised as a gifted dancer, writer, and artist, and I had lots of friends and boyfriends. But despite all this, I never felt like I belonged—and I never felt smart or accomplished enough.

The thing is, some of the events that block our soul are not only unseen by us but also undetectable to the world around us. For my part, being accepted by the outside world never quieted my need for isolation or solitude, or quelled my search for answers about why we are the way we are—or become who we become.

The First Whisper

Like many things in my life, my deep immersion into this work started with what seemed like a whisper.

Have you ever experienced something like that? An inner knowing or feeling that comes upon you like a soft breeze and makes you wake for a blink to acknowledge you have been touched, spoken to? It comes like a flash—a moment when the universe hugs you gently in preparation for walking you through the doors of something new and unknown. It's softer than a whisper, really. Kinder. A tender brush from nowhere.

The day the whisper came for me will forever be etched in my mind. We were having a Mother's Day / birthday party at my sister's house. It was a lovely gathering. But I was distracted, because my mother was very clearly not well.

The night before, she had been suffering from a stomachache. A bad one. When she'd said something to me about it, I'd told her she needed to start eating better.

That day at the party, I watched over her. Fixed her plates of food. Kept her hydrated. Worried, because she was not herself. My mother had never been a complainer, but I could see the pain in her face. I tended to her and tried to make her comfortable.

As I was getting into the car to go back to NYC, I turned to the video camera a friend was holding and out of nowhere said, "Well, this is the end of Mother's Day as we know it."

Somehow, I just knew.

When my oldest sister called a few days later and said Mom was going into the hospital for her gallbladder, the whisper came again: "*Your mother has cancer.*"

"They're going to find cancer," I told my sister.

"Don't be so dramatic!" she snapped back.

But sure enough, the news came the next day: my mother had a very rare form of cancer.

Eight months later, she passed.

One of my first successes in my professional life—landing a starring role on the celebrated daytime drama *As the World Turns*—was especially sweet because *ATWT* was my mother's favorite show. When I was sick as a baby, she would hold me and rock me while watching the lives of all those Oakdale characters, and as I grew older we'd watch it together religiously, week in and week out. Imagine our insane surprise, then, when in 1987 I landed a starring role on that very show. It was amazing, and a huge source of pride for my mom.

"I won't believe you've really made it until I see your birthday in *Star* magazine," she often joked with me over the next few years. In December 1991, it finally happened: the magazine printed my birthday in that month's issue. I brought it to my mother's hospital room, and we howled together about it.

Though we knew at this point that my mother's diagnosis was terminal, it was still a shock when she died four days later. My heart broke. She was my best friend, and the first person I had ever lost.

Still, even in the midst of my grief, I was aware that I was experiencing some of the greatest breakthroughs of my life in the months following her death. It was a "waking-up" period for me, so to speak; I knew my life and purpose were transforming.

It was the change the universe had been beckoning me toward.

Not long after Mom's death, I left *As the World Turns* and buried myself in the study of grief, change, transitions, and trauma. This loss—this first major and enduring heartbreak—was what launched me on my journey toward recovery from grief, loss, and unfinished business.

But it was only the beginning.

Finding the Rainbow

"Melanie, call me. It's important."

I was leaving a meeting with Arnold Schwarzenegger at a studio lot in the San Fernando Valley when I received that message on my VM. I had never heard my father's voice sound like that; I decided that it would be best to drive to my friend Lisa's house, which was only a few minutes away, to call him back. I had a weird feeling that this was not a call I should make on my little yellow Nokia while driving.

When I got to my friend's house to make the call, my aunt Ruth answered. My first thought was that something had happened to my aunt Edith, who was our family matriarch and quite elderly at the time. But when my father got on the phone and I heard the odd tone of his voice, I knew it was something else—something I needed to brace for.

"Hi, honey," he said softly. "There's been an accident . . ."

My whole body tensed. I waited.

"It's Roseann," he said. "She's dead."

My father's voice seemed to hit a different frequency as I collapsed. Lisa told me later that she heard me scream, and then saw me fall to the floor.

This was an entirely new level of grief and loss, beyond even the death of my mother. *This was a tragedy.* My sister was young and beautiful and full of life. How could she be gone?

When I was able to collect myself enough to ask questions, I learned what had happened: Roseann—my closest sister, eight years my senior, just forty-one years old—had dropped her daughter off at home after school that day and quickly jumped back in the car to pick up her son from his tutor's house, located only a few blocks away. As the sun set and my niece waited alone at home for her return, Roseann's car was hit by a driver who'd misjudged a stop sign. Her car hit a tree and she was killed.

What made all of this even more unfathomable to me was that I had just seen Roseann the Tuesday before, when she'd driven me into New York for a weekend trip to a wedding in the Hamptons with my boyfriend (soon to be my fiancé). We'd chatted and laughed the whole way, and when I'd arrived back in LA on Thursday evening I'd found a message from her waiting on my answering machine: "I heard about your engagement," she said in her bright, cheery way, "and I already bought my dress in a size four. I better stop eating now!" As always, she'd made me laugh.

It was 11:00 p.m. when I received that message, so I told myself to call her back the following afternoon. But I never spoke to my sister or saw her again. Friday, she was gone.

"I'll call her back tomorrow afternoon"—those words repeated like an echo in my mind, my heart, my soul, for years to come. Unfinished business.

Weeks after Roseann's death, I received a call from the

legendary Angela Lansbury, with whom I had worked previously on *Murder, She Wrote*. She was wonderful to me.

"My God," she said, "this is horrible. Come back and work on the show again. Let's keep you busy."

The first day I drove up to the set, a rainbow, clear and beautiful, was arched directly over the studio lot. Seeing it, I pulled over in my car and started to cry—but I wasn't sad. I was relieved. I knew Roseann was there with me in that moment, and it made me feel that there was nothing to be afraid of—that the emotions coming to me were a visit from my beloved sister, not simply painful memories. And what was allowing me to feel and honor that was keeping my heart open to the possibilities—not being busy or distracted. Not being closed or in resistance.

In that moment, I knew for certain that all the inner work I had been doing since my mother's death was working. I knew I was experiencing a blessing of presence, and it was telling me that what I needed was not to occupy myself but to *open* myself.

"Sometimes, the heart must break in order to open."
–MARK WOLYNN

This was a huge awakening for me. An experience of freedom, not of avoidance. Of joy, not veiled sorrow. And that's the moment when the distinction happened for me— the *insight*: the best thing I could do for myself, especially in a time of great pain, was to open, receive, and trust.

I had lost both my mother and my sister within four years' time. Though I was heartbroken, I came to the understanding that the reason we're here, in this lifetime, is to love and help one another. The finite time we have with the people we love is limited and irretrievable—but so often, we don't understand that until it's too late, or we are so mired in past heartaches that we can't see a way beyond the difficulties we're experiencing.

This realization is why, for the past thirty years, I've studied not just how we can survive the most difficult experiences of our lives but also how it's possible to thrive *because* of them. It's why I have dedicated my life to studying the art of finishing unfinished business.

The Life You Were Meant to Live

My story contains a lot of sadness—but my life has been rich with wonderful experiences too. I've gotten a chance to play so many wonderful roles: Emily Stewart on *As the World Turns*, Tora Ziyal on *Deep Space Nine*, Celia Morales on *Melrose Place*, Lucy Montone on *Curb Your Enthusiasm*, and Jerry's girlfriend Rachel on *Seinfeld* (who, famously, saw George's "shrinkage"), to name just a few. I've met, studied with, been mentored by, and loved so many amazing and brilliant people. My love of yoga and wellness has allowed me to improve the lives of thousands. Even more significant, I've had the opportunity to be a mother to my son, Gideon, my greatest teacher. And through nearly two decades of transformational coaching with individual clients and groups, I've given other people the tools to heal, grow, and reach their highest purpose. But more importantly, I've been *fully* present, entirely engaged, and profoundly in love with it all every step of the way. And that has only been possible because I've done the work to recover my soul from the past and complete the unfinished business of my life.

I want everyone to have a chance to experience the joy and peace of finishing their own unfinished business . . . and that is where this book comes in. Here, I've adapted the transformational techniques I have used in my own life, as well as in my one-on-one coaching clients and small group coaching program, into a program anyone can follow on their own or with a friend. The process will help you uncover the story of your life—heartbreaks, traumas, losses, impactful events, learned limiting beliefs, old behaviors and patterns, all of it. We will examine who your models and influencers were and are, and what relationships in your life remain unresolved and incomplete. We will discover how history and heartbreaks have impacted your choices, your behaviors, your relationship dynamics, your financial successes or failures, and even your health.

Through distinct steps and actions, we will organize your emotional life. We will distinguish the difference between *truths* and *stories*. We will get clarity around what should stay in your life and what you need to say goodbye to. By putting your heart in order, you'll declutter your mind, body, and spirit.

Saying goodbye to what's no longer serving you makes room for the best opportunities possible to enter your life fully. This process will help you understand the deep and profound connection between the mind and the body as well—how we cannot fully heal until we unearth what has been stored energetically in the physical body and soma (our experience of our body's inner and outer workings, as well as the boundaries and energies of the body—we'll go into this in more detail later!) as a result of past experiences. Remember, if your past remains unfinished, unresolved, and misunderstood, your present cannot change—and your future will pay an unimaginable debt.

Undertaking what I call the Unfinished Business Process takes you deep into your life and self so you can reach your highest potential in the future. Each step we'll take together over the course of this book will help you let go of your past and move you to completion and wholeness. You will know yourself as you never have before—at a heart and soul level. And armed with that clarity, you will be able to move forward into a life of peace and fulfillment.

When you complete the process outlined in this book, you will wake up to a future that is bright, open, purposeful, and filled with meaning—a life that was specifically meant for you. And the best place to start is by understanding exactly what unfinished business is.

Chapter 2:
Unfinished Business

I settled into a comfortable seat on my mat as the teacher *began her theme for the day's class. I hadn't sat in what she called a lotus position since I was a young kid. As soon as she started speaking, I started to feel deeply uncomfortable. I shifted myself, hoping to find a sense of ease again. My thoughts drifted backward. When was the last time I'd sat like this? With every word the teacher spoke, I felt more and more uncomfortable, as if I were about to pass out. I became almost claustrophobic. I began to feel nauseated and emotional, and I wanted her to stop talking. I shot up off my mat and went into the bathroom. I started to shake. I took some long, deep breaths and splashed cold water on my face.*

As I sat hidden away in the men's room, it all came flooding back to me.

I'm nearly nine years old. Today, like many others, my brother—three years my junior—and I put on our coats, grab the sled, and go marching up the steep hill near our house. We always ride on the sled together, but today I take my eyes off him and sit in the snow, legs crossed, fidgeting with my gloves and my boots. I look up and my brother is gone.

Down the hill, I see him. Still. He and the snow are covered in blood. I stand frozen. I don't know what to do.

After what seems like forever, my parents come out and find us. My brother is alive, but his hands are broken, his head needs several stitches, and he's suffered a severe concussion.

My parents never punished me or even talked to me about that incident again. It wasn't until I sat cross-legged on that mat that it all came back to me. I had never resolved or completed the experience I had with my brother and my parents that day.

That's what led me to do the deep unfinished business work it took to heal my heart and let go of the guilt and fear of the past. Now I do yoga every day . . . no bathroom breaks needed.

–JAMES

In the Gestalt Theory (Frits Perls, 1893–1970) there is a belief that human beings desire and *need* to make "meaningful wholes" from their experiences in life, and when the whole is not present we consistently seek completion. In other words, we fundamentally need to finish things and feel that snap of closure in order to make sense of our world and feel at peace in it. If we do not find this completion, the open-ended past lives inside us and pulls us out of alignment, leaving us searching for something we cannot even identify. Our fundamental nature as humans requires us to find closure for the past events of our lives, ranging from the minute and benign to the major and traumatic.

This premise also encourages us to remember that it is often impossible to "complete" certain situations at the time of occurrence. James's story is a great example of this. Due to his young age and his parents' inability or unwillingness to talk through what happened with him, there was no way for him to process the experience just after it happened.

When a challenging and grief-filled occurrence like the one James experienced that day in the snow remains unresolved, the incompleteness clutters our unconscious and expresses itself through mental distress and/or physical illness. The patterns or compensations we develop in our avoidance of completion can become a fixed shape or way of being in the world that can infiltrate all areas of our lives. In James's case, for example, his experience with his brother resulted in a pattern of avoidance. For decades after that accident, he tiptoed around all important discussions in his life—a compulsion that damaged his ability to develop deep, intimate relationships.

Until, that is, he did the work to shed that behavior.

These avoidances can become habits, especially if they are supported socially and culturally. In James's example, his family was happy to support a lack of communication and inauthentic behavior; they wanted to preserve the illusion that nothing ever happened and everything was fine. But that desperate need to avoid a feeling of pain we've experienced will train us to stay away from relationships and events that trigger us—which ultimately means quietly steering us into a life of feeling nothing at all. Those patterns and compensations dull our satisfaction in life, block our awareness, and diminish or even completely deny our psychological space.

Incomplete events and relationships take up far more psychological space than completed ones, and because of that they become the oars that row our psychological, emotional, and behavioral boats. Doesn't that ring true? I mean, have you ever lost sleep over things you have finished and feel good about?

We want to complete the incomplete. It is in our wiring.

With that in mind, it's not hard to understand that people with unfinished business tend to resent the past and are typically unable to focus on or live in the here and now, let alone build a dynamic future.

> *"Perhaps the biggest tragedy of our lives is that freedom is possible, yet we can pass our years trapped in the same old patterns. . . . We may want to love other people without holding back, to feel authentic, to breathe in the beauty around us, to dance and sing. Yet each day we listen to inner voices that keep our life small."*
>
> —TARA BRACH

Breaking the Loop

Years ago, I had a client, Sam, whose girlfriend left him after years of living and raising his three children together. They had been together for eleven years, and Sam had proposed to her many times, but each time she'd said no.

One evening, seemingly out of the blue, she came home and told him she was in love with a coworker and was leaving. Three months later, she married her coworker and got pregnant.

Sam had truly believed they had a great relationship and would be together forever. Then she left, and he never even spoke to her again. She never contacted his children. She never explained or apologized. He was devastated and deeply confused.

This trauma looped over and over inside Sam and his heart for years. When he came to me, he had not been able to commit to a serious relationship since that relationship's end—some five years previously. If he felt something for someone, he told me, he ran for the hills. Everything about him was stuck in this past incomplete relationship. Because he had not simply had his heart broken—he'd also been betrayed, deceived, left with the incomplete emotions of his children, and denied a full and compassionate explanation. He was emotionally overwhelmed, and his only learned technique for dealing with that kind of pain was avoidance and stoicism.

If Sam was to have any hope of moving forward and feeling whole again, he required full understanding of what had transpired, as well as total completion of the situation and the relationship. So that's where we started.

After doing the work to finish his unfinished business, Sam underwent a transformation: I watched him heal, shift, and, yes, fall in love again. He is now married and has two more children, and he has never been happier. But if he had not done the work to find completion for that previous relationship, he might have spent his whole life avoiding intimacy—or, even if he had found himself in a relationship again, his heart and soul would almost certainly have stayed blocked and uninvolved, leaving him to "phone in" his relationship and never feel deeply and truly loved.

What Is Unfinished Business?

Let's take a moment to get in touch with a basic example of how incompleteness impacts us and our minds, and to experience how it is our natural instinct even in the simplest and most elementary ways. Do you remember the draw-by-number books we all used to love when we were kids? Look at the picture below and see how your brain reacts. Notice what you do and how you feel.

Are you naturally completing it in your mind? Are you searching for the number 1? Don't you instinctively want to pick up a pencil and finish the tree?

Notice what you feel in your belly and heart, and what is going on in your mind, as you look at this image. Our minds, by nature, want to finish the unfinished—and, interestingly, so do our hearts and souls. There is such a feeling of satisfaction when we close the door and feel total resolution and completion with whatever is at hand, whether it's a drawing, a task, a relationship, or anything else.

Unfinished business is something that a person needs to deal with, work through, or complete. It is when anything—a relationship, a dream, an identity, or a familiar way of being in our life—ends due to circumstances beyond our control. It also includes the events we *react* to in unexpected and out-of-control ways (even when we have convinced ourselves otherwise, and even when the situations themselves are within our control). Basically, it's anything we need to say goodbye to or let go of so we can reclaim freedom for our hearts, minds, bodies, and well-being. It is this clutter in our psychology, physiology, and *soul* that makes us feel stuck or hooked into energy from the past, even if that past was yesterday afternoon.

The unfinished business that occurs throughout our lives typically gets buried down deep inside of us and remains there—until it starts showing up in our behaviors, choices, reactions, relationships, illnesses, and outcomes. Unfinished business shows up everywhere in our lives and robs us of our ability to make conscious choices in our day-to-day existence: how we spend or save our money, what kind of food we eat or overeat, opportunities we take or resist, the love we attract or repel, and more. It can steer us into addictions and lead us to waste our vital, precious energy on bad habits and repeated negative patterns of behavior. It keeps us from fully expressing ourselves and from living the authentic life, full of truth and integrity, we long to live. It takes us out of the present moment and disconnects us from ourselves and others. It charges us up (in a bad way) and gets us traipsing around in our past looking for answers or the original questions. It is an energetic force that blindsides us and moves us in the direction of a future we never intended; it is the saboteur of the now; it's life's biggest buzzkill!

Think of unfinished business as a sleeping dog deep in your soul and psyche that, when awakened by situations and triggers of the present, begins to bark and snarl, stopping you from full engagement, intimacy, action, or connection to the self.

Here are some common examples of unfinished business that we can all relate to:

- A family member or loved one died.
- Your parents divorced.
- Your boyfriend or girlfriend broke your heart or betrayed you.
- Your family pet died.
- You got married or had a baby and lost your carefree identity.
- You experienced financial hardship.
- Your marriage failed and your dream of a happy nuclear family was lost.
- You lost a loved one to COVID-19 and never got to say goodbye.
- You lost your career or business because of COVID-19 and you feel scared and out of control.
- You fell ill or were injured.
- Having children was your greatest dream, and you weren't able to have them.
- You got fired from your job.
- You got stuck in a job you're unhappy with.
- You have bad family relationships or history.
- You experienced abuse, neglect, or abandonment.
- You were teased as a child and have never regained a sense of self-worth.
- After graduating college, life turned out to be harder than you thought it would be.
- You became very successful, but when you did, your relationships changed for the worse.
- You always wanted your parents' approval but never got it.

- You were a latchkey kid and had to be an adult at far too young an age.
- You have a learning disability that no one has ever fully understood.
- You've never quite fit in.

Or how about this: life just hasn't turn out the way you planned, even after all the effort and training and passion and love you've put into it.

There are a million and one large and small things that happen to us through the course of our lives that have a huge impact on us and on our outcomes, most of which have hidden emotional and energetic implications.

> *"Trauma is a fact of life. It does not, however, have to be a life sentence."*
> **–PETER A. LEVINE**

Can you add a few of your own? Take a moment to ask yourself these questions:

- Have you ever found yourself in a situation where you wanted something or someone—badly—but you could not let yourself move forward, put yourself out there, or fully commit?
- Have you ever started falling in love and then suddenly started exhibiting self-sabotaging behaviors, ruining your chance to experiencing deep, enduring intimacy?
- Is there a career you've always dreamed of having, but it's seemed so far from reach that you've never attempted to go the distance—either because you don't believe you have what it takes to make it, or

because someone or something in your past made you feel like you weren't good enough?

- Does the world just seem too big and scary for you to even try?
- Do you find yourself making decisions based on old family beliefs, stories, and superstitions that don't belong to or resonate with you any longer?
- Do you struggle with decisions of any kind or commitments to anyone or anything?
- Do you hold beliefs about yourself and others that keep your world small and unfulfilling?
- Do you consistently repeat old patterns or make the same mistakes?
- Do you feel compelled to constantly prove yourself out in the world, never feeling successful enough, rich enough, or smart enough?
- Do you struggle with money and your beliefs around it?
- Do you have a hard time being kind to yourself or do you struggle with confidence and self-esteem?
- Do you suffer from anxiety, depression, or confusion about your life and its direction?
- Do you fight to lose weight or commit to self-love and -care?
- Do you struggle with a sense of distracted and depleted energy or deep conflicted emotions?
- Do you simply feel heartbroken?

As you can see, there are many ways in which unfinished business can show up in our lives. That's why I prefer the term "unfinished business" (UFB for short)—because it encompasses *all* the impactful experiences and events of our lives without cherry-picking which types are more critical or more important. No loss, change, transition, or heartbreak should be compared to another; they should *all* be investigated, understood, cleared up, and completed. But first you have to identify the experiences from your past that are currently impacting *you*.

Chapter 3:
Under the Unfinished

I thought this program was nonsense at first; the process sounded like voodoo magic or a silly game—until I did it! My husband and I had been trying to conceive a baby for ten years and had suffered many losses in this area of our lives before I finally got pregnant with my son, Connor.

When Connor died in utero after carrying to full term, I was beyond devastated. Beyond. The day I lost him, I held him in my arms until it was time to say goodbye forever.

For years that loss consumed my heart and thoughts. I felt like a failure, and I didn't even understand why. Then I did the work, and through this process I was able to transform a day I saw as traumatic into a magical day where I got to hold my son, see his face, and spend time with him. I gained a deep understanding of myself, my history, and my buried beliefs. Today, I'm so grateful for that.

On what would have been Connor's second birthday, I went out and celebrated his life instead of mourning and hiding away. My husband and I now spend our lives helping others heal from this life-changing, heartbreaking experience. There are absolutely no words to explain the dramatic shift that occurred for both me and my husband after going through this life-changing process.

–SARA

....

When my mother died of cancer at the age of seventy, it was a completely different experience than when my sister was tragically killed a few years later. My mother's death, though profoundly heartbreaking, was not a complete surprise. She was beautiful inside and out, but she was a heavy smoker, she ate poorly, drank dark liquors, never exercised, worshipped the sun, and had already survived two strokes, a cardiac arrest, and breast cancer.

My sister, on the other hand, was only forty-one years of age, was the mother of two young children, was not a smoker or a drinker, and had never really been sick a day in her life. My mother's death was a powerful loss—but my sister's death was a full-blown tragedy.

I continued to function through both of those experiences—surprisingly well, in fact—but underneath, I was not the same person and I knew it. Each loss showed up differently in my body, in my mind, and in my behaviors, and both losses remained incomplete in me. I was so confused by the duality I was experiencing: high-functioning on the outside, collapsing on the inside.

I wanted to know what was going on at the root of all this—under the unfinished. So I began to study relentlessly. I sought out specialists, teachers, and healers. I went back to school. I took on apprenticeships with experts in different healing modalities. I dove in headfirst.

In doing so, I learned things about grief that might surprise many people. I began to understand that the beliefs people and communities who have suffered high-impact loss and grief events carry put serious limits on them and their recovery. There is a sense of collective defeat. They learn to embrace the false idea that they must carry their pain and heartbreak forever; they believe people when they tell them,

"You know, you never really get over it, but you can learn to cope with it"; "Keep yourself occupied"; "Stay busy"; "Give it time"; "Try to move on—try to let go"; "Eventually, you'll think about it less."

These beliefs are not true. You do not have to *bury* your history, tamp it down, run from it, or wait it out. You don't have to play mental games while carrying dark feelings deep inside. You don't have to merely *cope* with loss, grief, change, heartbreak, and unfinished business. You don't have to suffer for the rest of your life.

> *"When you're trying to survive, you turn malady into a coping strategy and loss into a culture."*
>
> **–STEPHEN JENKINSON**

Hardship is not a handicap; it is an opportunity for growth. It is a doorway to deep wisdom. These experiences are injuries of the soul and to the energetic system, and, just like physical injuries, they must be healed before you can truly move on and live your life with dignity, delight, and joy. You can complete the past. You can design the future you want.

Unfinished Business Is Universal

We all carry beliefs around hardship and loss that are imprinted upon us by our families and the societies we live in.

Take Sara, whose story you read at the top of this chapter: Her family had a silent undercurrent of belief that if a woman couldn't have a child, she was a failure. Sara, without even realizing it, took that belief on and carried its weight along with the heavy loss of her baby, Connor. Until she woke up to the fact that much of what she was feeling didn't even belong to her but rather to her family, her recovery felt nearly impossible.

These unconscious ways of being that we have inherited from our families of origin, our ancestors, and the constructs of greater society, as well as the internalized emotions brought on by and held beneath the surface of our incomplete high-impact events, can keep us imprisoned in the past. The stories we were told early in life are the stories we are still telling ourselves and others—even after all the growing and adulting we think we've done!

Once these created or inherited stories, behaviors, identities, and limiting beliefs are internalized, they take root in the *subconscious* and become energetic blocks that bend our souls off course, preventing us from creating lives of purpose and meaning. These energy blocks prevent change and healing and cause us to doubt our effectiveness in the world. They prevent us from hearing our own intuition—the internal compass we all possess that is meant to lead us to our own North Star. They cause us to confuse our inner *critic* with our inner *voice*. They can make us feel lost and without guidance. They can hijack our intuition and point us in the absolute wrong direction.

It is not until we bring these energy blocks into the light, uncover what is under the unfinished, and then begin to unpack and question them that we can release them and help our cleared energy take root in a new and fertile ground.

What Is Grief and How Is It Connected to UFB?

When loss of any kind impacts our lives and our nervous system, we can experience discordant and confusing emotions. Together, these feelings of confusion and discordance are what I refer to as *grief*.

At its root, the desire to finish unfinished business—the impulse to search for peace, healing, and self-discovery—is brought on by our earliest losses . . . loss of loved ones, loss of trust, loss of self, loss of self-worth, loss of safety, loss of control or faith, and so many others that we will address in this program. This also includes experiences of change or transition where we are forced to let go of familiar people, patterns, or things that we've held dear and counted on throughout our lives. This includes changes we typically see as positive—weddings, graduations, children leaving the nest and starting their own lives, starting a family, or experiencing a great success.

It's important to understand that these are not only deeply emotional experiences but also psychological, neurobiological, and physiological experiences. Furthermore, grief does not present in a simple linear fashion; my years of studying grief and loss have shown me that it manifests more as a constellation of energy, one that moves differently for each person and each experience. Though we may all go through some or all of the emotional categories many grief experts tend to talk about, in my experience there is no particular order that happens in, and there are more categories than are typically discussed. For example, my constellation of grief presented in a totally different fashion when my mother died than it did when my sister was killed. When my mother died, I was able to carry on and stay productive, help my dad, and make career choices. When I learned that my sister had been killed, I collapsed—and then started showing up for my life in a whole new way.

When we experience loss of any kind (from small disappointments all the way up to full traumas) the nervous system works to find a new equilibrium. Think of it this way: Have you ever traveled somewhere, perhaps a place you knew in your childhood, and when you arrived everything was different? Perhaps the buildings were gone or changed, or the neighborhood had been turned into a commercial district—and now you found yourself standing there in total confusion. You did your best to figure out what used to be where; tried to recall the exact placement of each of the old structures. You were truly disoriented. You kept revisiting the past in your mind, attempting to make sense of where you were now.

That emotional loop—that feeling of not being able to align or match things up—is similar to how we experience grief.

This is when your brain comes in and tries to intellectually solve the problem. The brain tries to use reason to reconcile the discordance by working with the "story" to either change, justify, explain, or make sense of the past. Our clever brains try to intellectually bypass, manage, or even outsmart the pain and confusion—an intellectual trick that, unfortunately, serves only to bury the event deeper in our bodies and somas. Remember this: you cannot *solve* a feeling; you can only shift the way you think about a feeling. And in order to do that, you need to look honestly at *what* you're thinking and the *way* you're thinking about it.

Here is the truth: In order to move on completely—in order to turn crisis into experience and wisdom—we must release the old, derive meaning from it, and find purpose and connection in the new. We must help the nervous system adapt to its new reality.

"Embrace your grief. For there, your soul will grow."
–CARL JUNG

This means we cannot just replace something or distract ourselves by keeping busy, taking drugs, self-medicating, tamping our emotions down, self-affirming, or waiting for time to pass and "make it all better." To find peace, we must complete the incomplete and find the *whole* again—actively.

Here is one big reason that unresolved grief and heart-break can be so life-damaging: it is *exhausting* to our system. We keep our guard up for fear of the pain that truly caring about something or someone again can bring; we stop allowing ourselves to be vulnerable in the face of the unknown; we become hypervigilant; we try to bury or "cope with" painful and stressful emotions. And doing all this uses up tremendous amounts of energy. For Sara, living in this way wore her down; she felt a constant, low-grade feeling of hopelessness and depression, and she struggled with malaise and a revolving door of common (but depleting) illnesses.

Unfinished business is also cumulative. Left untended, it eventually creates what I call an "emotional hairball" in us—one so immense that we cannot cough it up. The temptation is to tamp it down. That temptation must be resisted. The only way to get rid of that hairball once and for all is by pulling it apart, examining it, figuring out what it is and why it's there, and then releasing it from our system.

One of my clients, Bill, was an Ivy League, highly polished, uber-successful entrepreneur and businessman. His face was stoic and certain; his hair and demeanor were as polished as his oxfords. But Bill had experienced profound losses—he had lost both a child and a spouse tragically to suicide—and under that suave exterior, I could see his pain loud and clear.

Like so many who experience such tragic losses, Bill thought he was beyond help. "I'm here because you come highly recommended—but I don't think you can help me," he told me during our first conversation. "As a matter of fact, I'm certain you can't."

As his words might indicate, Bill came to me full of resistance. He believed that holding on to the pain was, in essence, the same as holding on to his lost loved ones. He came across as smart, successful, put together, and "in control," but he was shattered inside and didn't know how to put the pieces together again. Like so many people I've worked with—and so many others out in the world, suffering in silence—he was resigned to the "fact" that he needed to get on with his life and accept that nothing would ever be the same again.

Bill and I worked together for about six months, and then we went our separate ways. I felt we'd made great progress, but I wasn't sure what would become of him next.

About a year later, I was sitting in my office when my assistant told me I had a visitor and ushered a vaguely familiar man through the door.

It took me a moment to recognize Bill, because he looked *completely* different. He seemed relaxed, at peace. His entire wardrobe was different. Even his *hair* was more relaxed—no longer combed back and shellacked as it had been before. And his face had taken on a soft, even cheery, countenance.

"I don't know how you did what you did, Mel—I just know my life changed," he told me, the disbelief evident on his face. "I'm in love again. I'm happy. I am at peace."

We laughed together, and he gave me the warmest of hugs before we said goodbye. It was a magical experience for me, seeing how far he'd come—to see him thriving, enjoying life, after he'd spent so long merely surviving.

If you find yourself uncomfortable in your own skin or life; if you find yourself constantly seeking to gain someone else's approval, or expand your bank account, or acquire a fancier car or smoother face or tighter body—there's deep work to be done. To be clear, there is nothing intrinsically wrong with money in the bank, fancy cars, and being admired! You can still have those things, if it's what you truly want. But first you need to find the *real* you, and figure out what you truly desire. And that can only come after you've done the work to unearth those truths.

Not All Grief Is the Same, but It All Matters the Same

As I said in the last section, no two clients I've worked with have ever shown exactly the same constellation of grief symptoms. (In this context, I'm using the word "constellation" to mean a group or configuration of ideas, feelings, characteristics, objects, and energies that are related in some way; I am not referring to Family Constellation therapy.) I like to think of grief as a constellation because it is not a singular, "fixed-star" experience; rather, it takes on different shapes and forms. We all perceive impactful events differently and handle them differently. We also hold them in our body differently. There is no one magic point of release for everyone. The work in this book that you will do is specifically created to help you find and release *your own* specific combination of grief and heartbreak.

> *"You can't go back and change the beginning, but you can start where you are and change the end."*
>
> –C. S. LEWIS

How the Unfinished Business Program Is Different

There are so many different and wonderful philosophies and programs to help us heal, and my program honors, addresses, and even incorporates parts of a number of them. What sets my program apart is that I focus more on the "whole"— on the healing of the soma. This is critical because loss, change, transition, and heartbreak are energetically stored in the subconscious, as well as in every cell of our body. In her book *The Molecules of Emotion*, neuroscientist Candace Pert explains that our cells, muscles, and tissue carry our memories in detail. In other words, our traumas live in each cell of our body—"Our psychology becomes our biology." Our body and soma hold our past; our (conscious) mind memorizes it and then tries to cope with it. Or, as Bessel van der Kolk, a trauma guru and brilliant teacher I've had the honor of studying with, says in his book *The Body Keeps the Score*, "As long as you keep secrets and suppress information, you are fundamentally at war with yourself. . . . The critical issue is allowing yourself to know what you know."[1]

It is for this reason that the UFB approach is holistic and integrates the entire being, moving you into full awareness of yourself from a mind, body, soma, and soul perspective: in this way, we allow ourselves to know what we know—and only then can we release it.

Chapter 4:
Understanding the Whole

For years I struggled to advance my career. I had no idea why I felt so inadequate and could not accept promotions without feeling like a total imposter. I had this haunting feeling that I was on the wrong path—totally out of sync with my life and with myself.

I came from a family of boys, and being the only girl took a toll on me. I was close to my brothers and my dad, and we had a lot of fun together, but I could never run as fast, hit as hard, or throw as far. I made every team I tried out for, but deep down I knew I did it for my dad and my brothers, not for myself. I wanted to fit in, be accepted, and be loved. I missed out on many things I really wanted to do. I was musical, artistic, creative, and very feminine. But I never pursued the things I loved. I pursued the things that helped me belong.

Imagine being stuck between being a "not good enough" boy and not knowing who you are at all as a girl. I was an imposter all the way. I knew I had to come full circle with the confusing beliefs I held about myself. I had to reconcile the conflicting inner stories and inner struggle between who

I was expected to be and who I was meant to be—who I wanted to be.

After I completed the Unfinished Business webinar it was like a veil had been lifted. I felt totally empowered. I went back to school, I changed companies, and the next promotion I was offered I grabbed with both hands! I am now an executive at a niche cosmetics company, and I've never been happier or felt more like myself. In many ways, I don't even understand how it all worked. I just know that it did.

—CAROLINE

....

This all may seem like a lot to parse out, but I want you to think of this chapter as a guide—a glossary of terms, so to speak. Think of it as reference material to pull up whenever you get stuck on a concept or a word as you move through the text. Do not get nervous if you don't understand each one fully or know them all by heart. You simply need to have a basic understanding of the principles and concepts regarding the *soul,* the *conscious mind*, the *subconscious* mind, the *Three Brains Theory, bioenergetics*, and the *soma*, because we're using all of these philosophies/ modalities for the work we'll be doing together for a reason. As we conclude our work together, you will understand, simply by following the process and by doing the work, that they all fit together to create the "whole"—the Gestalt, the completion.

Since this book is about healing trauma, it seems important for you to have a working definition of what it is, so I will also define that term here (to the best of my ability; it's a tricky one!).

As you read this chapter, I recommend that you use a highlighter to mark the places that feel most important to you so you can use it as a reference tool as you continue on into the chapters that follow. Each time a term comes up in the book, if you need a reminder of its meaning, pop in here and refresh your memory with these quick and basic definitions.

Soul

> *"The most powerful affirmation doesn't come from the conscious mind but from your Soul, an affirmation in which you are not trying to convince yourself of something you don't believe, but rather you are becoming aware of the truth and the reality of what you truly are."*
>
> **–DRAGOS BRATASANU**

"Soul" is a word we all hear frequently yet for which we rarely receive a satisfying definition. Merriam-Webster defines it as "the immaterial essence, animating principle, or actuating cause of an individual life" and "a person's total self," among other things.[2] A speaker at a conference I once attended, meanwhile, shared this definition, which she attributed to cultural historian Thomas Berry, PhD: "The soul is the primary organizing, sustaining, and guiding principle of a living being." A beautiful concept, yes—but a vague one.

I like to explain it this way: The soul is our purest awareness, or consciousness, which is the state of being awake and fully perceptive. When this consciousness is in its most alert, unstressed form—when the mind is clear and all inner chatter is quiet—you are experiencing *Soul*.

Here's an example: Think back to when you were young. Remember how when you go outside to play with your friends at this age you are completely engaged, lost in imagination and connection? Then, suddenly, the spell is broken as, out of nowhere, your mother calls, "Dinner! Time to come in and wash up!" You think to yourself, *Dinner!? I just got out here. What's she talking about?* Only then do you realize that hours have passed like minutes. As you run inside, you look behind to see your creations and the aftermath of your play—a snowman, a fort, tire marks from your new bike, the broken branches of the tree you just climbed, the smiles on your buddies' faces. You give them a quick shout—"See you tomorrow!"—and then run inside, blissfully content.

That's you experiencing soul. It's the unencumbered and creative part of the self that is the reason we search and aspire to greater things. That feeling of oneness with everything and with nothing at all outside the deep sensation of your own beingness. It is the flow state—the self in its purest form—like what we see in the Michael Jordans and the Pavarottis in this world.

Thinking of our soul's energy expression and how it can be disturbed, redirected, or blocked brings to mind light reflection and refraction. In reflection, when a light ray strikes a smooth surface—let's say a mirror—the light bounces off of that surface at an angle equal to the angle at which the incoming ray hits the mirror's surface. This is called the law of reflection—"the angle of incidence equals the angle of reflection."[3] Refraction, on the other hand, occurs when light hits something that is not so smooth or has obstructions. When this happens, light will change its speed and the light ray will bend either toward or away from what is called the "normal line," an imaginary straight line that runs perpendicular to the surface of the object. The amount of bending, or what's called the angle of refraction, of the light wave depends on how much the blockages or obstructions slow down the light or perhaps halt it completely.

This is how our energy system and our soul respond to the density of our internal clutter, the weight of our unfinished past and the ragged edges of our old, worn-out myths—they are moved off their natural course, bent in an unintended direction.

Today, science is finally understanding how our *subtle body* energy, or *energy anatomy* (the various energetic layers that make up a human being beyond its physical form), shapes and informs our structure, thought processes, health, and happiness more than they ever realized. There is also an increasing acceptance of the idea that most illnesses have an underlying emotional root. With that in mind, it is reasonable to say that when we fail to clear away what our body and spirit no longer need and heal the places within us that are laden with open-ended sorrow, we literally block the nature of our *soul*'s intelligence. We distort and refract our innate wisdom, losing the ability to hear the one true voice that should be our guiding compass: our soul.

The Conscious Mind

"Intellect takes you to the door, but it doesn't take you into the house."

–SHAMS I TABRIZI

The conscious mind is the seat of our intellect; it is our active awareness or the state of alertness we develop to pay attention to the things we feel and think as we go about our lives. It gives us the ability to perceive, feel, or be conscious of events, objects, or sensory patterns. It's the part of the mind that collects our data. It contains all the ideas, thoughts, feelings, and desires that we are *aware* of in any given moment. But our objective, "thinking" mind is not a multitasker; it can only hold one to three thoughts at a time. While it can call memories *in*, it doesn't *have* memories itself.

The conscious mind has four basic and essential functions:

1. It identifies incoming information through any of the six senses and consistently categorizes what is happening around us all the time.
2. It compares all our previous information with the newly accessed and received data.
3. It helps us analyze said data.
4. It accepts or rejects that data and makes decisions and choices.

Here's an example of the conscious mind at work: You've decided you want to lose five pounds. You buy a book, pick your favorite recipes, set up a meal plan, and even create a shopping list with a weekly meal spreadsheet. You move forward and follow your plan to a T, and it goes great.

This is the conscious mind in its most well-organized and committed state. Hold that thought . . .

The Unconscious Mind

"Our heart glows, and secret unrest gnaws at the root of our being. Dealing with the unconscious has become a question of life for us."

–CARL JUNG

The unconscious mind is where all our past experiences are stored. It consists of the processes and systems that occur automatically and are not available to introspection or reflection. It holds repressed feelings, automatic skills, subliminal perceptions, and automatic reactions, as well as hidden phobias and deep desires; it has the capacity to learn and process information. The main job of your unconscious mind is basically to store and retrieve data.

Your unconscious mind is also in charge of ensuring that you respond to every event in your life in exactly the way you are programmed to respond. It makes everything you say and do fit the pattern or patterns that reflect your "self-concept"—your idea of the self, built on the beliefs you hold combined with the concepts of others. It retains a perfect record of all your comfort zones and fights to keep you in them. Any time you try something new, you can feel the pull of the subconscious, urging you to return to the status quo. It's the reason that even contemplating doing something different from what you're comfortable with can make you feel anxious, tense, and uneasy.

Your unconscious mind is subjective. It is not responsible for the reasoning in your life. It simply receives and obeys the commands of the conscious mind—or, at least, it tries to. Let's go back to the garden analogy we have been using. Think of the conscious mind as the gardener: it plans the garden, it tills the soil, it plants the seeds. Your subconscious mind, in this metaphor, is the soil in which the seeds are planted. Growth occurs, or doesn't, depending on the condition of the soil.

Back to the "losing five pounds" analogy from above: You have been doing great with your new regimen; in fact, you've been following it strictly for eight weeks. But today is your brother's forty-fifth birthday party, and the whole family is there. Mom made your favorite puff pastries and an ice cream cake. There are chips, dip, and homemade calzones.

What happens? You know! And even if you do manage to resist all that tasty temptation, take a moment here to envision the struggle and hear the thought patterns telling you how hard it is to resist all that delicious food. Maybe you tell yourself you've had a hard week and deserve a treat. Maybe your thoughts go more toward how you're doomed, like most in your family, to be defeated by weight forever.

That's an example of the unconscious mind at work. We want the familiar. We want the comfort zone. This is the part of us that believes the familiar bad is better than the unfamiliar anything. This is the part of the mind that makes change so very difficult.

The Three Brains Theory: How Our Body Communicates

"You have to master not only the art of listening to your head, you must also master listening to your heart and listening to your gut."

–CARLY FIORINA

Let's take a moment to understand how the different areas of the body talk to each other. It's crazy to comprehend, but many behavioral scientists today agree that our body has three different brains. Marvin Oka, behavioral change expert and author of *MBraining: Using Your Multiple Brains to Do Cool Stuff*, explains the concept this way: "Why are we calling these brains? We are not calling these brains. Science is calling these brains. There has to be a technical definition to what makes a brain a brain. Your elbow is not a brain. Your kidney is not a brain (as far as we know). But there are lots of good reasons why science can actually show that the head, the heart, and the gut are brains. They have their own intrinsic nervous systems. They've got neurons. They've got the whole range of capabilities that complete complex adaptive processes. They can take on information, process it, store it, change, and adapt. Basically, if it can learn, it's a brain. Lo and behold, these different brains do different things."[4]

So, yes, we have not one but *three* brains—I call them the Royal/Ruler, the REAL, and the Root Brain—and we are only just beginning to understand how profoundly they rely upon one another.

1. **THE ROYAL/RULER** brain resides in our head. It is the master of processes such as thinking, perception, and cognition.
2. **THE REAL** (Relationships, Emotions, Affection, and Love) brain is our heart. It is where our values lie, along with the process of emoting and valuing, as well as the way we feel about relationships.
3. **THE ROOT BRAIN**, the oldest of the three, is our gut and is responsible for our identity, safety, and protection. Our gut is extremely important in the functioning of the immune system. It takes care of self-preservation, fear, anxiety, mobility, and action. It sends the information it experiences and feels up from the root of the soul, through the core, and up to the crown of our soul. The Root Brain is where it all begins—and began.

Our gut and our heart are constantly communicating with our cerebral brain. These messages are constantly being exchanged between these areas as pure energy. The heart and the gut are not as chatty as the cerebral brain, however, so their words are brief, and they use metaphor as a guiding tool. These communications or signals can even be thought of as *felt talk* or *felt thought*; they might communicate with sensations or with single words like "hurt," "shame," "ugh," "yuk," "ow," and "stop," among others.

As I mentioned earlier, we are made of energy, and when energy is blocked—from grief, trauma, heartbreak, anything that might be thought of as unfinished business—somewhere along the path from the gut to the brain, the pain gets stuck as well, preventing communication from taking place and distorting or muting our intuition. Learning to really hear, decode, and understand what *all* our brains are trying to say is a skill that is fairly easy to cultivate but totally changes the game. Learning to *body listen* will allow you to reclaim your deep inner knowing and to recognize, understand, and follow the voice of your soul.

Bioenergetics

"Bioenergetics is an adventure in self-discovery. It differs from similar explorations into the nature of the self by attempting to understand the human personality in terms of the human body. Most previous explorations focused their investigations on the mind."
–ALEXANDER LOWEN

Bioenergetics is a field of study, grounded in biochemistry and cell biology, that concerns energy flow through living systems and the transformation of that energy in living organisms. Simply put, bioenergetics deals with the biology of energy exchange between and within living things and their environment. It's a system of alternative psychotherapy that is based on the belief that emotional healing can be aided through the resolution of bodily tension—that releasing blocked physical and psychic energy can lead to healing and improved well-being.

Believe me, it's way less complicated than it sounds.

Bioenergetic therapy works with the *whole* person. It addresses the conflicts in all areas of an individual—cognitive, emotional, and physical. Through this form of therapy, individuals increase awareness around old patterns of behavior, as well as their actions and reactions in their daily lives. Bioenergetics also allows you to release the negative emotions and feelings that are often the root cause of disease and energy blockages. This increased awareness and unblocking leads to an increased ability to tolerate and resolve old conflicts and traumas and frees up your energy system so you're better able to experience pleasure, joy, fulfillment—all the best parts of life.

The Soma

"If you want to find the answers to the big questions about your soul, you'd best begin with the little answers about your body."

–GEORGE A. SHEEHAN

The soma is where a person perceives bodily sensations and somatic experiences and is distinct from the soul, mind, and psyche. Derived from the Greek word *soma*, meaning "body," the soma is the cell body or, as one of my teachers once quoted Candace Pert as so aptly having put it, "the cells, muscles, and tissue that carry our memories in detail." It is the vessel in which everything we have been discussing in these last few pages is housed; it is the physical body *and* our experiences of it.

As I mentioned earlier, the body and soma hold our past; our brain memorizes the stories they hold, reinterprets them, and then tries to cope with the meaning and messages it derives from them. The soma is how we experience our own bodies' inner and outer workings, as well as the boundaries and energies of the body; it's the mind's ability to perceive the body. Whereas the body is simply the physical body, the soma is both the body and its experience of itself—the body in its wholeness.

Bringing It All Together

It is vital that you understand the distinctions between these six terms and have a general idea of how they impact us before you begin this healing process, since they will be brought up throughout this book. The soul, the body, the subconscious and conscious mind, the three brains, and the soma are all part of the process of healing the heart and soul. In the chapters ahead we will be working in all of these areas.

Lastly, let's talk about trauma.

Our understanding of trauma—what it is and how to define it—is ever evolving. Most traditional experts struggle with how to define it outside of PTSD, and many acknowledge it only around events of great and obvious magnitude: war, school shootings, witnessing gruesome circumstances, and so on. However, these are not the only events that cause trauma—not even close.

At its most basic, one might say trauma is the emotional response that results from experiencing a distressing or life-altering event that damages a person's sense of safety and self, as well as their ability to regulate their emotions and establish healthy relationships. But I believe it is both more complex and more subtle than that.

I've heard trauma guru Peter Levine describe it like this: "Psychological trauma can happen to anyone when they perceive a situation as a threat and are unable to complete a satisfactory fight, flight or freeze response." In his book *Healing Trauma: A Pioneering Program for Restoring the Wisdom of Your Body*, he goes deeper: "In short, trauma is about loss of connection—to ourselves, to our bodies, to our families, to others, and the world around us. . . . It can happen slowly, over time, and we adapt to these subtle changes sometimes without even noticing them. These are the hidden effects of trauma, the ones most of us keep to ourselves. We may simply sense that we do not feel quite right, without ever becoming fully aware of what is taking place; that is, the gradual undermining of our self-esteem, self-confidence, feelings of well-being, and connection to life. Our choices become limited as we avoid certain feelings, people, situations, and places. The result of this gradual constriction of freedom is the loss of vitality and potential for the fulfillment of our dreams."

Trauma specialist and psychiatrist Bessel van der Kolk defines it this way in his book *The Body Keeps the Score*: "Being traumatized means continuing to organize your life as if the trauma were still going on—unchanged and immutable—as every new encounter or event is contaminated by the past."

These are wonderful explanations. There is, however, an important point that I would like to add: trauma is not defined by the size or nature of the event but instead by what happens inside of us as a result of that event. In other words, trauma is what lives inside the person, not the event itself; it is not the story of what *occurred* but rather the pain and terror that event imprinted upon the person who lived it.

Over the course of these next chapters, we will open ourselves up to the vast understanding of the soul; mine the mind; dig in to the body and its energy currents; and move through the layers of how the stories we tell ourselves and others impact our mind, body, and soul. In doing so, we will begin to eliminate all the blocked or frozen energy that has been weighing us down, stifling our growth, and impacting our choices and the distribution of our power—freeing ourselves to move on to the next level.

So, what are we waiting for? Let's dive in!

Chapter 5:
Program Overview

When I was four and a half, my father left us. One day he was just gone. What I remember of him is not negative. However, its echo in my memory is sad and dark. My father spent most of his time in his room when he was home. He was a gentle man. He was always kind, but he never really engaged with me or my sister. Sometimes people would come to the house to talk to my mom, and my dad would just sit there in silence.

Years after my father left, when I was in third grade, our teacher, Mrs. Roberts, asked the class what we wanted to be when we were older. So many answers came out of our young mouths: a scientist, a pro ballplayer, a lawyer, a ballerina, a TV producer. I blurted out, "I want to be a psychiatrist."

I remember thinking, Why did I say that?

Mrs. Roberts seemed very proud of my answer, however, and so did my mother when she heard, so I stuck with it. I got into great colleges and eventually graduated AOA from a top medical school.

I must admit, I hated every minute of all of it. I would wake up in the night sweating and asking myself, "What am I doing here?" But there was some deeper pull to stay with it and I refused to let my mother down—so I powered through.

I practiced medicine for nearly twenty years, in fact. Eventually, though, I fell into a deep, unending depression. I was prescribed many meds to help me, but nothing worked.

It wasn't until I started doing the Unfinished Business work that something shifted. In researching my past, I discovered my father didn't just leave; he was put into a mental institution and shortly after died form an aneurysm (or so I was told; to be honest, I'm not sure the aneurysm part is true). What struck me so profoundly about this journey was the realization that even as children we are so deeply aware of what is happening around us. It may not be a conscious awareness, but it steers our life and our choices regardless. My fascination with mental illness, I suppose, was really a deeper need to know my father.

I am no longer a doctor. I am a science writer now. I love my work, but I never would have allowed myself the freedom to choose this life if I had not completed the past that had such a deep and powerful hold on me. My mother passed before I got here, but I know she would be proud of me and the path I have chosen. I think Mrs. Roberts would be too.

–ANU

First, I want to say I'm so glad you're here and ready to move ahead with the work. Second, I want to make a couple of things clear: 1) there is no way to do this work incorrectly; 2) some of us may have more complicated or heavier issues to process, and everyone should go at their own pace.

If you stay committed, shifts *will* occur—so take a deep breath, know you're in the right place, and let's move forward.

This book is not a piece of material you can casually browse through or complete in a week. The program contained in these pages is a step-by-step *process* meant to be worked through on a weekly (or longer, if you need more time) basis. The reason for this is that the body and subconscious mind need time and space to digest the material and the shifts that will take place as you move through the program. Rushing just doesn't work.

This process is designed to be gentle yet effective. For each step, you will read a chapter and complete assignments. Please do not take it upon yourself to jump around; for the process to have its fullest and most profound effect, you must proceed chapter by chapter. Let this book be your guide and companion to a place that may, as of now, feel uncharted, but someday soon will be familiar terrain. Trust the work, follow the steps, be kind to yourself, deal with your unfinished business, and change your life once and for all. Healing can really be as simple as that.

Through this process, you will uncover the story of your life—losses, heartbreaks, learned beliefs and patterns, and all. You will examine who your models and influencers were and are, as well as what relationships and unfinished business in your life remain unresolved and incomplete. You will discover how the past has impacted your choices, your behaviors, your relationship dynamics, your financial successes or failures, and even your health. You'll develop an understanding of the deep and profound connection between the mind and the body, and how we cannot fully heal until we unearth what is stored energetically in the physical body and the subconscious mind from past situations and unresolved "felt thought." You will organize your emotional life, sort out and distinguish the difference between truths, lies, and stories, and find clarity around what must stay and what must go so you can eliminate unfinished business and make room for your highest potential and purpose. And finally, you will complete the past, regain your true inner power, and call your soul back *home*.

Again, aside from following the steps in sequential order, there are no rules here. Make this book your own. Let down your defenses and embrace the journey. This requires that you trust—me and the process, yes, but mostly yourself. It also requires your unfiltered and unguarded honesty. No one else is going to read your responses or judge you. And *you* shouldn't judge you, either! This program is not a form of punishment. It's not meant to shame you or make you feel bad about yourself. It's about one simple thing: getting to the root of the problem. That's why the extent to which you are real with this process will dictate the extent to which you heal.

What to Expect

I don't want you feel like you're driving blind without knowing where you're going; it's always nice to have a general sense of the direction you're headed in and an idea of what landmarks you'll encounter along the way. So, without going into too much detail, here's an overview of what to expect in the coming chapters:

1. **IN STEP 1** of our prework (Chapter 6), we will discover who we are and why we feel, act, and think the way we do. We will unearth and examine the past and present. I call this "tilling the soil"—getting our garden ready.

2. **IN STEP 2** of the prework section, we'll take a good look at the "I Wish" stories we have been carrying with us on our journey—the stories we have been telling ourselves and what we "wish" we could have been or should have been.

3. **IN LESSON 1** (Chapter 7), we will begin to define our memories in terms of models, mantras, and

long-held beliefs, as well as how our culture, society, and support systems keep those behaviors in place and thriving. Examining these helps us to see why we are the way we are and where we get / have gotten our data. These are learned thoughts, beliefs, and behaviors—they are not who we truly are or who we are meant to be.

4. **IN LESSON 2** (Chapter 8), we will begin to identify the way we respond to the world around us to gain approval and acceptance from our family, loved ones, peers, and even strangers. We will also learn to accept responsibility for our actions and circumstances so we create a *destined* life rather than fall prey to a *fated* one.

5. **IN LESSON 3** (Chapter 9), we will locate the *charge* and triggers that expose the blocks and stuck energy in our body, and take a hard look at the way we have creatively coped with heartbreak, change, loss, trauma, and grief.

6. **IN LESSON 4** (Chapter 10), we'll begin to curate and categorize our heartbreak and unfinished business. We'll look at the various types of heartbreak and loss, without retrenching or retraumatizing ourselves.

7. **IN LESSON 5** (Chapter 12), we'll chart our heartbreaks one relationship at a time. We'll examine closely our significant relationships and examine the various paths to letting go. We will learn to fully own our lives while beginning the process of completely forgiving the past.

8. **IN LESSON 6** (Chapter 13), we'll release our past unfinished business and the patterns of behavior that surrounds it. Through the process of clarifying and clearing, we will let go of the

blocks that have long held us back. We will also learn about transactional writing and its power to heal and complete the past.

9. **IN LESSON 7** (Chapter 14), we'll reframe and recode our past so we can move on. We will "Write the Wrongs" and envision the authentic, soulful future we long to create. (This is an important and vital step in moving on to an empowered life—the one originally meant for you.) Then we will redesign and rediscover who the "true you" is so you can become who you were meant to be all along.

10. **FINALLY,** we will learn tools and practices to carry the process forward and to keep our hearts, souls, and lives free from future clutter.

Please commit now to completing all the work in this book. The ROIII (return on inspiration, illumination, and investigation) will last a lifetime.

Things to Keep in Mind

Over the course of this journey, you will experience shifts in your perspective on trauma, heartbreak, disappointment, old beliefs, change, loss, and transition. You will learn new concepts and fresh awareness. You will start to understand how the past has been encroaching on your present and future life. This work requires you to be totally honest, open, nonjudgmental, and compassionate. Please show up for yourself and offer yourself support, love, and acceptance as you complete these lessons.

In every lesson to come, there will be homework assignments, exercises, reading, and reflection questions. Each one will end with a moment of Higher Self-Talk—an offering, prayer, meditation, or conversation of sorts between you and your higher self. These sections are meant to connect you with a higher source of energy—with the world around you. Think of it as a conductor of current; it should inspire you, remind you of what is possible, and give you a chance to express your gratitude to the universal energy that connects us all. Feel free to use my words or to create your own when you reach these sections!

If you should meet any challenges along the way, please be gentle with yourself and remember that there is no wrong way to do this work. At the same time, if you start to get behind in the work or need to take a break at some point, please do not let too much time pass before continuing the process. Make a deep commitment to yourself to keep going. Do not be hard on yourself, but do make a true and solid commitment to follow through to the end.

You are welcome to use this as a buddy system or group process as well. If you choose to do so, please be certain you completely trust and feel free to be totally open and honest with the people involved; feeling closed off or anxious will stunt the work greatly. Please also honor the fact that no one is there in the role of counselor, judge, or leader. You are together to create a compassionate space, full of love and kindness, in which healing can occur—nothing more, nothing less.

Above all, it's imperative that you *do the work*. Every assignment matters and informs the process, so don't skip anything. As you begin to complete these lessons and enjoy the discoveries you're making, you'll get used to the cycle and hopefully fall into a routine. Ideally, you'll set aside one to two hours each week to do the work to give yourself the space to open and shift.

This work is deep, meaningful, and life-changing; trust the process, and you will succeed. I am so proud and honored to be on this path with you.

Now let's get moving . . .

Part II

Chapter 6:
Rethink

I was a football star in high school, and when I graduated I was given the opportunity to play for four different colleges on scholarship. It would have been a full ride. No one gave me advice about what to do or where to go to college, or if and where I should accept a full scholarship, and ultimately I decided to play for one of the bigger schools to be near my friends. Honestly, I didn't think it through. The school I chose had players way better and way bigger than me. I didn't play often enough and when I did, I frequently got injured. Because I felt second rate, I became an angry player, and my temper impacted my game.

I was a good student, and I completed my business degree. I never got any offers to play ball professionally, so I went into business for myself. I founded a very successful cabinetry company, and I took great pride in my work. But then, when I was around the age of thirty-eight, I started to feel very depressed. I felt like a failure. I kept replaying my early life choices over and over in my head. I wished I had chosen a different school, I wished I'd controlled my temper and sought guidance for how to handle my negative emotions. I told myself over and over that I'd blown it—that

I would never be happy now, and that if I had only done it all differently, I would have gone pro.

The idea of self-forgiveness—of letting go of the past and clearing unfinished business so you can be fully present for your life in the now and create the future you desire—was so new to me when I began my Unfinished Business work. I didn't even think I could do it—but then I did. And in doing the work, I opened my eyes to what and whom I needed to forgive that I'd never even realized—my dad, my mom, my coach, but mostly myself.

I had to dig deep, but I am truly at peace now. I love my work. I take great pride in my success. And I have not said the words "I wish," "If I'd only," or "I should have" in years.

—PATRICK

In most of us, there is a broken heart waiting to be heard and healed. Every one of us has experienced times of difficulty or disappointment; every one of us has experienced some form of trauma. And to protect ourselves from suffering, we try our best to deny or ignore those painful experiences and memories, sometimes to the point of "forgetting." Even when we're trying to heal, we believe deep down that we are incapable of bearing the pain. We stuff our feelings and memories back down into our subconscious minds and bodies. However, when we ignore our past in one area, it inevitably shows up in another. And just because we've decided we do not want to face something does not mean it has agreed not to go in search of us.

Avoiding our past pain in the present is an ineffective way to deal with those experiences; it often prolongs our suffering and shapes our lives in a myriad of damaging ways. Our heartbreaks are a reality that need to be dealt with because every hurt, every resentment, every pain we stuff down continues to live in our body at the cellular, somatic level. Bessel van der Kolk named his book *The Body Keeps the Score* after this phenomenon. In that book, he explains, "Neuroscience research shows that the only way we can change the way we feel is by becoming aware of our inner experience and learning to befriend what is going on inside ourselves."[5]

Basically, whether we want to address our past or not, it will find its way into every cell of our being. As award-winning science journalist Donna Jackson Nakazawa says, "Your biography becomes your biology"[6]; our heartbreaks are never far away—it's just a question of whether we're looking inward to find them. But just as this heartbreak is present in every cell of our body, so is the deep understanding and desire of the soul to lean toward happiness, health, and possibility. We just have to do the work. We can turn the light on and start this journey at any moment we choose; no matter how recent or distant a heartbreak may be, a remedy is always there for the taking.

When we become aware of the limiting beliefs, unresolved relationships, incomplete stories, myths, and wounds of our past, we can start to act with compassion for ourselves and others—we can begin to use our energy for forgiveness. And when we do, this energy will embrace us, heal us, and free us from the history that no longer serves us.

The next five lessons are deep root work; we're going to be doing a lot of digging. Think of this section as preparing the ground, so to speak. We'll be pulling out the weeds of our garden by their roots, and analyzing the soil and environment in which we've been planted. *Why?* Because the way we are raised and the environment we've spent our lives immersed in affect how we receive, perceive, and process data, as well as how we hold and distribute our energy.

The purpose of this lesson's work is to get to the bottom of what you are tolerating (rather than working through) emotionally, what triggers your uncomfortable emotional states, and what unfinished business you're holding onto. We're going to dig down deep to unveil our most impactful traumas and unfinished relationships, and any old or misunderstood stories that still weigh us down energetically, psychologically, and physiologically. This exercise is to help you unearth what is reaching up from the past to grab your subconscious and somatic (physiological) attention and prepare you to start looking ahead to the future with fresh eyes. You're going to till the soil of your garden, churning old and buried events of the past up to the surface and into the light of awareness.

Prework: Tilling the Soil

✵ PART 1: JOURNALING

Over four consecutive days, spend fifteen to twenty minutes—*no more than that*—writing down your deepest feelings and memories of the emotional, impactful experiences that have influenced your life the most. These can be related to health, body image, self-respect and dignity, heartbreak, loss of a friend, death of a pet, loss of a home, a surprising or traumatic transition, a divorce, or even happy, life-changing events like the birth of a sibling, graduations, becoming class president, or winning the lottery. Include anything and everything that has truly impacted your life, whether in small or large ways. (Please reference the Holmes and Rahe test in Appendix 1 to help your understanding of what trauma, loss, and transitions are and how many we can experience in a lifetime.)

In your writing, be completely honest and totally free. Explore how the events and upheavals affected you. Get in touch with your most challenging feelings and thoughts about what happened and how you felt about it, both then and now.

These events may come from your childhood, relationships with your parents or other loved ones, significant relationships of any kind throughout your life, career or health situations, even things that society thinks of as good or exciting that may have felt very difficult or life-altering for you. You can also include global experiences that have impacted you personally, such as your experience with the COVID pandemic.

As John F. Evans and Dr. James W. Pennebaker, professor of psychology at the University of Texas at Austin, write in *Expressive Writing: Words That Heal*, "Writing is a potentially effective method to deal with traumas or other emotional upheavals. The research evidence is indeed promising." They go on to say, "Writing about traumatic experiences for as little as twenty minutes a day for three or four days can produce measurable changes in people's physical and mental health. . . . Expressive writing can positively affect people's sleeping habits, work efficiency, and their connections to others."[7]

Even if writing does not come easily to you . . . keep going! Don't worry about your handwriting (or typing), spelling, or grammar. Keep in mind that this exercise is different from typical journal writing or diary keeping in that you will only do it for *four days in a row* and only for *twenty minutes per day.*

Set aside a time and a place where you can be alone and undisturbed. Write continuously for fifteen to twenty minutes and with awareness that this is only for you—no one else ever needs to see this. And finally, don't overstep your own boundaries. If you feel unready to write about something, please respect your feelings and wait for the correct time.

I use the tool of writing this way—for just four days in a row, for a short time at each go—because going over and over past events for an extended period of time can be detrimental to one's mental and emotional health. As Dr. Pennebaker writes, "There is convincing evidence that writing about the same topic in the same way day after day is not helpful and may possibly be harmful. You can analyze something too much."[8]

Pennebaker looks at this type of writing as a "course-correction mechanism" and believes it should not be an extended practice as you risk getting into a sort of "naval-gazing" or a form of self-pity. However, standing back every now and then and evaluating where you are in life is really important.

Tips for this writing exercise:

1. Find a place where you feel safe, comfortable, and peaceful.
2. Make certain you will be without distraction for at least fifteen to twenty minutes.
3. Write with awareness that this is only for you— no one else needs to ever see it.
4. Let your writing flow freely. Enjoy the self-expression. JUST WRITE!
5. Write only about things that you feel have been extremely impactful upon or meaningful to you.
6. Keep your body relaxed—and don't overstep your own boundaries.

After you've written for four days in a row, I want you to list the *top three to five events* that stick out to you. They could have been difficult to write, or perhaps they came too easily. They could also be something unexpected—something that came to you once you started writing that you didn't think would come up. They should feel significant. You will know them when you feel them. Circle the events, highlight them, or put a star next to them—not because they're better or more important than other events you wrote about, but because they were likely more *impactful*, for whatever reason, and therefore can reveal a lot about the stories and pain you're carrying around with you.

✺ PART 2: WISHES THAT DIDN'T COME TRUE

Let's take a moment to review your writing exercise in Part 1. Take note of any "I wish" stories attached to your impactful events, as my client Patrick did. Investigate what you believe your life might have looked like if it had gone differently or as "planned." Go all the way back to kindergarten, summer camp, first love, first job. Pinpoint the moments, regrets, and relationships you still hold stories around.

So many of us don't even realize we are hanging on to old stories. It is time to make a conscious effort to examine them. Pay attention to the beliefs you have around these events. Do you think your life would have been better? Do you feel like you missed out? Do you sometimes think, *If only I hadn't made that mistake?* Pay close attention to what you're feeling in your body, head to toe. Note any feelings of regret, loss, anger, or shame. Take your time. You can use the chart on the next page (visit www. unfinishedbusiness/worksheets to download and print), or your personal journal.

I Wish:

It Would:

If I:

We/I Would:

Now that you've done this, let me point something out.

We can't move forward until we let go of the old and fully embrace where we are standing in the *now*. Everything we are carrying around is *heavy*. And it matters. It *is* matter! Light can't penetrate that burden; that's why we remain energetically stuck.

We can't lighten our load until we identify the unfinished business we're carrying around and get rid of it. In the lessons to come, that's exactly what we're going to do.

Homework Follow-Up

Before we move on, here are some questions I want you to use as prompts to gain even more clarity around the writing you've done this week. Once you have completed the above exercises, write down your answers to these questions:

- What emotions came up for you while writing?
- Were there any emotions that shocked you?
- Were there some new memories that came up as you began to write?
- Were you surprised about anything you still wished for?
- Did any new awareness bring on sadness, regret, or relief?
- Did you feel energy move in your body during this exercise? Where?
- How did it feel to write about those memories? Does your body feel differently after writing them down?
- Was there an event that when you wrote about it, without embellishment, you began to rethink how you perceived it in the past? Did that change your feelings about the event?

Higher Self-Talk

Becoming aware of my past and forgiving myself and others for it is an act of grace. Though this work may be new and challenging, it has been a powerful experience to write from the depth of my heart and soul about the experiences I've had that have impacted me most deeply. My life has been complex and made up of so many experiences—some in the shape of heartbreaks, losses, traumas, and change. Good or bad, light or dark, I accept the truth of my past and I am proud of myself for the work I did this week. I am ready to move on and to understand who I am at a deeper level. I am eager to learn what is no longer mine to carry, and to embrace the courage it requires to release it all in the present. The time has come to feel clarity and certainty in my life and to commit to moving toward a bigger, brighter future. I am fully open and receptive to this work. I accept the sensations of any energy that may be waking and shifting inside me. I am excited and hopeful for all that will come next. I feel deep gratitude toward myself—for showing up, and for the grace of an open heart.

Chapter 7:
Lesson 1

*M*y dad was a hardworking, quiet, immigrant busi- nessman. He was humble and he mostly kept to himself. He had a workshop in the basement, and he was a wonderful musician. Several of my parents' friends, in contrast, were very successful and confident businessmen with big personalities—very different from Dad. My father had very strong beliefs around success and money that were almost the opposite of his friends. Things like, "You never talk about money, you never show you have money, and people who do are braggarts and showoffs." Things like, "Hard work and a 'nose to the grindstone' attitude is the only way to a gentleman's success." My father died a tired man, and though we lived a comfortable life, at the end he had little to show for his years of hard work. I've come to understand that in many ways my father was intimidated by real success and power.*

As I got older, I started to notice my own discomfort around the highly successful men in my life. At dinners or meetings or conferences, I refused to talk about money. I also judged the people who did, and the people who wanted to have a lot of it, quite harshly. I had a thriving seven-digit business in the world of real estate investments, but I felt stuck. I mean really stuck. It kept me up at night. I won-dered why I couldn't get to the next level so I could retire and enjoy my successes. Or why I never really felt proud of all my accomplishments—why I just kept working and spoke to no one about what I'd achieved. All my friends were respected business leaders, but I shared nothing of what I was going through.

Finally, my wife told me I needed to figure things out so we could start actually enjoying our lives.

I jumped into the UFB process, and all the beliefs and stories I had buried in me about work, money, business, and success came to the surface. It was mind-blowing. I was carrying my dad and his Old World values and beliefs everywhere—beliefs and behaviors that no longer fit the paradigm of the modern-day businessman, and no longer applied to me, my life, or my world.

It was amazing to me that for all these years I'd been modeling my father and his beautiful but antiquated way of being. To be honest, I felt guilty at first about the idea of letting them go—but I worked through it all, and it has been life-changing in so many ways. Monetarily, emotion-ally, relationally, and, quite frankly, spiritually. I continue to use this work in my life and with my employees today. Sometimes you just can't see what's holding you back from your best life. But when you do find the answers, even if they are from the past, your whole life can change and level up in the blink of an eye.

–JACK

There comes a time in all our lives when we need to self-actualize, realize our full potential, develop our abilities, and become everything we are capable of becoming, free of the narrative created by our past and the people in it.

Over the course of this chapter, we will develop a deep understanding of why we are the way we are and what we must do in order to become the people we are meant to be. Only then can we finally begin to experience the joy that comes with living as our true selves.

Why We Are the Way We Are

The way most of us function in the world post-adolescence is a learned way of being. We are not born like this. We came to be the way we are because of the influences and influencers around us that figure most importantly (or prevalently) in our lives. In this chapter, we are going to take a serious look at how *the daily models of our past become the silent mentors of our future.*

Here we are going after the origin of the deeply held beliefs, patterns of behavior, and self-limiting stories that, like prerecorded tapes, repeat over and over in your mind and show up in every aspect of your life. We will also be examining the support systems and voices that keep these conditions alive and well. These behaviors, beliefs, and patterns act as an acquired way of being in the world, a sort of internal blueprint on how to live, function, and react to life's circumstances. These models, mantras, and beliefs are not real, though they are very real to you—to all of us.

Our childhoods shape us; they imprint us with the map we use to navigate our way through a complicated and ever-changing world. The beliefs, identities, and ideas we're told to embrace become our own personal compass. But that doesn't make them true.

Though it may be hard to believe, everyone's reality is not the same. Not even close. Each of us has a reality custom-made by the systems and ways of being we learn from our early examples and models. We have no choice in picking our family of origin. Nor do we have any control over the factors that drive family behaviors and dynamics in our early lives; those have absolutely nothing to do with us. Yet these behaviors and dynamics are what shape our lens and color how we see the world.

> *"The brain is a historical organ. It stores our personal narrative."*
>
> –BRUCE PERRY

Models, Mantras, and Beliefs

As children, our very survival hinges on acceptance by our family and community of origin. We have to organize our behaviors, therefore, to comply with the rules—spoken and unspoken—set forth by the authority figures around us.

The silent behaviors and patterns that are our learned ways of being are what I call *models*. The verbalized slogans that we hear consistently are our *mantras*. And the quiet undercurrents that seem to direct our choices, behaviors, and actions from the depth of our being, without the involvement of the conscious mind, are our *beliefs*. This is where the webbing of the roots beneath the surface of our garden begins.

In an effort to belong, children internalize the rules of behavior—at the cost of their true selves—from their earliest years. The models, mantras, and beliefs we are exposed to in childhood can envelop us and, without us even realizing it's happening, become our primary points of reference for how to live our lives. They become our identity, internally and externally, and can steer us toward or away from life's circumstances or even freeze us in place, making it impossible to grow.

When the pain of the loss of our original self has nowhere to go, it can get redirected against the self in the form of depression, self-doubt, self-destructive or self-limiting actions, aggression, and a consistent sensation of heartbreak or misalignment. Look at my client Jack and his struggle getting unstuck, not even realizing he was acting out the beliefs, fears, and limitations of his father. This lack of self-awareness infiltrated his life, business, and marriage, and nearly crowded out his happiness and success.

These models, mantras, and beliefs shape our relationships with ourselves as well as with other people. It stands to reason, for example, that if you grew up in a home or in a community where people made you feel deeply loved and important, your inner compass tells you something is off when people in your life today do not honor you in the same way.

Models, mantras, and beliefs also create our personal expectations of what we deserve and what we can and will accomplish; shape our habits and actions; and, ultimately, dictate our self-worth. So if we grow up in a home where we are ignored, teased, unseen, unheard, unloved, or simply crowded out, our inner compass is pointed in the wrong direction. Our sense of self and self-esteem is marred by shame, contempt, pain, loneliness, and humiliation—and that makes us more likely to think of unhealthy relationships and mistreatment as being justifiable, acceptable, or even normal. As a result, we have a hard time moving into or even identifying a better version of life, because we don't feel capable or worthy of such a life. When we lack the proper modeling for success or follow-through, we can spend our lives feeling incompetent or less than others who had positive modeling during their developmental years.

Every family has its upside and its downside—its light and dark. Many of the heartbreaks we experience in our developmental years are unintended or even imperceptible, and even the "happiest of families" can have heartbreak at their core. This second step of the process will help you to identify the limiting beliefs, mantras, and models from your family of origin—and they are there, even if you had what you considered to be a happy childhood—and guide you in reorienting your inner compass so it points in a healthier, more self-loving direction.

✸ MANTRAS IN ACTION

Tammy's father, Paul, was a funny guy with a bright personality and a successful career as a lawyer. Everyone loved him. When at home, however, he could be tough—his expectations of his children were high.

Tammy was an artist; she excelled at the creative. She was just average in the world of academics, however, and Paul believed the only path to success was a graduate degree and a straightforward professional path. He treated his daughter's art as a hobby, not a career. Tammy's mother, meanwhile, was a quiet woman who told Tammy to "Do as your father says."

So Tammy learned to downplay her art, and although she felt inadequate at school, she forged ahead with a business major in college and eventually became an advertising executive. But despite her apparent success, she struggled with the inner heartbreak of self-betrayal and an abandoned dream. She had a hard time with money and the idea of *real* success.

These are some of Tammy's mantras as learned from her father:

1. "Art is for children."
2. "Artists are poor."
3. "Only special people make it as artists."
4. "Who do you think you are, Picasso?"

5. "When are you going to grow up?"
6. "You're different, Tammy. Try harder to fit in."
7. "You don't have what it takes. Get a job or get married!"

Tammy heard these mantras daily, and she took them with her wherever she went. If she saw an ad for an art exhibition or passed a museum and felt the pull to be involved, she would hear the mantras: "When are you going to grow up? You don't have what it takes!" When she struggled with money, and she still thought of herself as a secret artist, she would think to herself: *Artists are poor; get a job or get married!*

The mantras she heard from her mother also greatly impacted her life:

1. "Do what your father says."
2. "Your father knows better." (Implied: men know better; you can't trust your own judgment, etc . . .)
3. "Marry someone who can take care of you and let art be a hobby."

With these mantras echoing in her mind, Tammy had a hard time making her own decisions and trusting her own instincts about her life. She consistently asked for others' guidance and suffered from high levels of anxiety when on her own in the world. But when she finally decided to do deep work on herself and faced the fact that she had the soul of an artist, her life took a dramatic turn. She is now a highly successful graphic artist and painter and makes her living strictly from creating art—and she no longer lives by the mantras that held her back for so many years.

"When we stop doubting, and start believing in our new life, we start behaving as if it's possible—and we ultimately become it."

–DR. JOE DISPENZA

✺ MODELED BEHAVIORS IN ACTION

When I was a child, I walked out on the back porch of my house one day to find my mother sitting on the stairs crying. I knew it was bad that I had walked in on this private moment, and I knew it would never be discussed afterward. I wondered why she didn't want anyone to know she was sad, why she didn't want a hug, and why she couldn't just speak her heart out loud. She was my mother, though, so—thinking that she must know what was right, smart, and good—I went back in the house and never mentioned it to anyone. But I never forgot the unspoken lessons I learned that day.

In my home, we kept matters of the heart to ourselves until there was a fight, or until we told each other the truth through teasing or some other form of humiliation. We never just spoke the truth openly, calmly, or honestly in the moment. As I grew up, after getting things wrong in many relationships I had, I started to see how I carried that old story, those old behaviors, and that early modeling with me—and how doing so was hurting me and those I loved.

These are some of the modeled behaviors I learned from my family:

1. When you are hurt, sad, or upset . . . deal with it alone.
2. Be strong for others, but don't be a burden when you're hurt.

3. Vulnerability is threatening.
4. It's not dignified to fall apart. Be stoic.
5. Strong people don't need, they are needed.

These behaviors became deeply rooted within me. Though I was the one everyone in my life turned to, it took me years to learn how to be truly vulnerable or to ask the people who deeply loved me for help myself. Never showing my fears, sorrows, or weaknesses felt right to me—but it also left me feeling lonely and unsupported.

After doing my own UFB work, my life expanded greatly and so did my relationships. I don't feel the need to do everything on my own or to "act" as though I have everything under control anymore. I share my heart. I show up completely—warts and all.

✸ BELIEFS IN ACTION

Beliefs are a tribal or personal set of internal rules. They are an ideology—a set of principles and tenets that make up our philosophy for living. Once internalized, they guide our reality and rule our world. They can be passed down from generation to generation, or they can be an amalgam of many different beliefs quietly combined within a family or group. They are the foundation for the way we function. They *can* be spoken or modeled, but they don't need to be in order to influence us. Beliefs exist within families, cultures, communities, and social constructs. They are the undercurrent that pulls us along without our conscious awareness.

My client Connie comes from a family of immigrants. Her mother does all the housework. She also works hard running the family business. She shops, cooks, and makes everyone's clothes. Connie's father does not help in the home and only works certain hours. He comes home for lunch, which Connie's mother prepares for him, and is home by five each day for dinner, which is always put promptly on the table. Connie's mother never complains about this arrangement. In their culture, women are second-class citizens and expected to speak only when spoken to. Those words are never said in the house, but they are taken as a fundamental rule. Yes, there is some modeling here, but the beliefs are also quiet and generational. They go without questioning. They are a truth that has seeped into Connie's choices, actions, and beliefs about herself and the world.

We'll dig further into how these beliefs have played out in Connie's lived experience in the homework section we're about to begin.

Lesson 1 Homework: Identifying Your Models, Mantras, and Beliefs

"For some of our most important beliefs, we have no evidence at all, except that people we love and trust hold these beliefs. Considering how little we know, the confidence we have in our beliefs is preposterous"

–DANIEL KAHNEMAN

Now that you have a sense of what models, mantras, and beliefs are, you are going to look through the window of your childhood and find the models and mantras that shaped *you*. Remember, we are looking for a collection of things that were said, done, not done, deliberately avoided, or expected in your developmental years and beyond. Family rituals and superstitions will also be included here. The laws and realities you unquestioningly live by today were formed a long time ago, and we need to examine them without holding back.

Anything and everything that seems to fit these categories should go down on paper. Don't question yourself. I recommend carrying around a small notebook, and when you hear yourself saying something that sounds like a parent, a sibling, or someone else from your life might say, either now or in the past, ask yourself: *Is this a model, mantra, or belief that was passed on to me? Who is in my brain? Whose words are coming out of my mouth?*

Keep a list going all week. You'll be amazed at how many you'll discover in just a few days!

Using the chart below, begin to make your list.

Just to reiterate, here are what models, mantras, and beliefs are and some examples for you:

- **MODELS:** what you *saw* in the behaviors around you, spoken or unspoken, that shape your behaviors and beliefs today.
  - EXAMPLE: Connie's mom does all the household chores, manages the schedule, runs a business, and helps her parents too—that's her role in the family as mother and daughter. Connie takes everything on herself and has never understood why she struggles to ask for help.
- **MANTRAS:** the *spoken* beliefs and expectations that shaped you and still show up in your life now, directing how you deal with the world around you.
  - EXAMPLE: Connie often heard statements like "Your mother will do that" or "A woman's place is in the home" when growing up. Today, she feels she's better off doing [chore, cooking, schedule, work, parental care] herself so it gets done and done right.
- **BELIEFS:** the ideologies or principles that make up our underlying philosophy for living.

○ EXAMPLE: Connie struggles with feeling empowered or deserving. She has never stood up for herself. She's always given her power over to men in relationships, and she is finally understanding why this has been such a struggle in her life.

- I want to add one more thing to think about here—your *origin* and its *support system*. In other words: Who initiated these patterns in your life, and who supports them today?

  ○ EXAMPLE: Connie's mother initiated a pattern that the wife/mother/female authority takes on most of the household labor and oversees the household. She always said, "A woman's work is never done." Today, there are lots of people around Connie (friends, family, but especially her boyfriend) who allow and encourage her habit of doing everything and not delegating chores that do not require her personal touch—that could be done by literally anyone.

Something to remember is this: although I've broken these into separate categories, one can bleed into the other. For the purposes of our work, please trust your instincts. And do not leave out any of the family/cultural/religious superstitions and traditions you carry, even if they seem small or innocuous; beliefs, rules, guidelines, structures, and traditions should all be included.

Use the chart example on the next page (download and print at www.unfinishedbusiness/worksheets, or sketch out your own on a piece of paper, to get started):

MODELS	MANTRAS	BELIEFS	Origin & Support System
(FATHER) Follow the traditional path. Men are sensible women are not. Work hard. Always be likeable. **(MOTHER)** Women are quite and well behaved. Do as you are told. Get married and be a good wife.	"Art is a hobby not a dream to follow." "You are not good enough." "You are like a child." "Get a real job." "Find a man to support you." "Don't make waves." "Try to fit in, Tammy"	Following your heart is childish. Be a good girl to get love. Women are powerless. Life is hard so play it safe. Learn to fit in.	**(O)** Mom and dad. **(S)** Mom, dad, principal, boyfriends, boss.

Homework Follow-Up

Now that you've reviewed all your models, mantras, and beliefs, I want you to take a moment to assess which ones are holding you back, which ones you already know to be untrue, and which ones you can identify as beliefs in need of real investigation:

- How does it make you feel to discover/uncover some of these beliefs?
- Are there any models, mantras, or beliefs that have harmed you over the years? That have kept you "in your place" or away from your dreams— that may have served other people, but not you?
- Name all the places these ideas and messages show up in your life.
- Are there any in particular that have you feeling stuck?
- Are there any you now identify as loops or negative voices that repeat in your head as thoughts or show up in the world as stories you tell?
- Do you recognize any phantom conversations, arguments, or fantasies you tend to run over and over in your head when alone?

Higher Self-Talk

I am more than the stories I have told myself and more than the stories I have been told about myself and who I should be. I am more than the familial laws and beliefs that have been passed on to me. I now know that I can release the negative, limiting beliefs and old, worn-out tapes from the past that I've been holding onto and replace them with new and inspiring voices for my future. These voices will support my growth toward my highest self and greatest potential. I sit in grateful awareness of the old stories, models, mantras, and beliefs that do not serve me, and now have the wisdom to distinguish my true self from the mythical mantras and models of my past. I have the power to change the old mandates that have been running my show and operating just under the surface for years. I let go of the false with compassion and I welcome the truth with love. I now have information I didn't have yesterday, and that is enough for today.

Chapter 8:
Lesson 2

I never told anyone I was gay—not my parents, not my siblings, not my friends, and most certainly not my boyfriend who ultimately became my husband. I knew my family and community were very religious and had strong feelings about homosexuality, so I became the perfect student, dressed beautifully, and made sure no one would ever guess that I was a lesbian. Frankly, I tried for most of my life to hide it from myself.

I went to an Ivy League college and graduated top in my class. While there, I fell in love with a woman. I hurt her very badly by denying myself and leaving her behind. Years after graduation and the start of a successful career in engineering, I got married to my longtime boyfriend. After we married, we struggled to get pregnant. I began to drink heavily. I hated myself. I secretly tried therapy, but even there I only told partial truths. I wasn't being honest about anything in my life. I just wanted to numb out and pretend I was fine.

I finally went to AA and got sober. A friend of mine who had done Unfinished Business work while he was in AA recommended that I try it. I desperately needed something to work, so I did.

I'm not going to lie. It was hard. I had so much shame, and I had been pretending to be something and someone I wasn't for so long that I didn't have any idea who I really was or what I was even looking for. But I found this work to be deeply compassionate and freeing. It's so crazy—when I finally came out and lived with total integrity, it was as if I finally made sense to everyone around me. Most importantly, I finally made sense to myself. I am at peace now, and though I still have things to heal from and discover, I am the closest to knowing who I truly am, and I feel more "complete" than I ever have in my life.

—ERIN

A small-time musician dies and goes to Heaven. He is met at the Gates of Heaven by St. Peter.

"Welcome, my son," St. Peter greets him. "Let me show you around."

They arrive at a door and St. Peter opens it. Inside is Eddie Van Halen, playing the guitar.

"Wow!" says the man. "I'm a huge fan!"

They continue on and St. Peter stops at the next door. Inside is Jimi Hendrix, writing a new song.

"Oh my God!" the man exclaims, eyes big as saucers. "It's really you!"

They continue on again and arrive at a final door. St. Peter opens it. Inside, Bono is recording a song.

"I didn't know Bono was dead," the man says, puzzled.

"Oh, he isn't," St. Peter responds. "That's God pretending to be Bono."

I know that's a silly joke, but it highlights the fact that no one is exempt from wanting to feel special, important, and, most of all, loved, admired, and respected for their gifts and their presence—not even, in this case, God.

Let's begin this chapter with the simple awareness that every one of us, on some level, has a deep need to belong. One of the worst feelings in the world is that of rejection, exclusion, or even going entirely unnoticed. Right? Isn't that why we all start our lives with fantasies of being a rock star, a world-class athlete, a prima ballerina, a tech genius, an Oscar-winning actor, or Pulitzer Prize–winning writer? We all want to be loved, admired, adored, and most of all fully accepted.

But *how*, exactly, do we want the world to perceive and accept us? What do we do to accomplish that? When we veil our true selves in order to be embraced by others, what is the cost? What have we lost in the process, and what must we recover? Those are some of the questions we will be investigating in this lesson.

The AACTs of Life

"There are many roles that people play and many images that they project. There is, for example, the 'nice' man who is always smiling and agreeable. 'Such a nice man,' people say. 'He never gets angry.' The facade always covers its opposite expression. Inside, such a person is full of rage that he dares not acknowledge or show. Some men put up a tough exterior to hide a very sensitive, childlike quality. Even failure can be a role."

–ALEXANDER LOWEN

In my early studies, I fell in love with depth psychology and the work of Carl Jung. I became deeply fascinated with his philosophy on personas in particular.

The *persona*, as described by Jung, is the social face we present to the world—the mask we create both to make a definite and designed impression upon others and to "conceal the true nature of the individual."[9] It's the idea that in public we present an exaggerated or manufactured version of ourselves in our attempt to belong or, even better, make an impression. These "personas," or what I have come to call AACTs—Acceptance and Approval Create Tricks—create a gap between the real, connected self and the artificial, created one.

The purpose of this week's work is to unearth and *identify* our AACTs—the personas, masks, or false identities we adopted in early childhood and beyond in order to survive in a world we were not yet skilled enough to fully manage—and all that we have abandoned in order to feel the safety of approval and acceptance. AACTs are a deep denial of our flaws, as well as a way that our beliefs and behaviors show up in our lives in our quest to be included, accepted, and loved. In other words, *acceptance and approval create tricks*. For all of us.

We will also investigate in this lesson which things we must take responsibility for, and examine what kind of shift must occur in order to create a *destined* life versus a *fated* life. These three pieces of our work this week fit together like pieces of a puzzle; when it's done, we will have a complete picture of the version of ourselves we present to the world.

In short, this week is about fully seeing the gap between who we are and who we present ourselves to be in the world—the version of ourselves that is obedient to outside expectations and pays excessive attention to what people think of us—and working to close that gap. This is one of our most difficult challenges in this process, but it is surmountable, and it is worth the effort.

Where Our AACTs Come From

Many years ago, I worked with an eye movement desensitization and reprocessing (EMDR) specialist. I was having a problem flying on airplanes after my mom died, and I was told EMDR could help.

This specialist was the first person to diagnose me with a particular form of dyslexia that shows up in people who are naturally left-handed but were forced to become right-handed (or at least that's the way I understood his explanation). This was a life-changing discovery for me. As a youth, though I did well in school, my teachers couldn't figure out why my reading was slow even though I loved it and my comprehension was high. This caused tremendous anxiety in me and made me feel I wasn't smart or quick-thinking enough. I developed an insatiable desire to achieve and to be seen as an intelligent, well-read, capable student. I became a voracious learner and reader—an overachiever. I developed an underlying fear that I would never catch up or be good enough unless I tried to be good at everything. This, the specialist said, is what he sees in most of his clientele.

Have you ever gone to a gathering and simply watched people, noting their different behaviors and learned ways of being? If you haven't, try it—it's fascinating. These outer characteristics come in all shapes and sizes, and they are there to keep us safe from rejection, judgment, and hurt. You see it every day on social media, right? Everyone has it all together; they all have the perfect life, face, body, job, "brand," you name it. And yet almost none of those stories are true.

The people who present themselves as the most gorgeous person in the room have the deepest bruise from feeling ugly, invisible, ordinary, shamed, or excluded from a young age. People who are the most organized or strive for perfection felt the most out of control as a child. People who present themselves as the richest and most powerful felt the most inadequate, weak, powerless, and rejected growing up. In other words, most people adopt AACTs to compensate for their most vulnerable areas. The poor child desires to be rich beyond comprehension. The abused child longs to be powerful. The abandoned child longs to belong and strives to be adored. The child rejected by their peers longs to be popular—or they may relish coming across as aloof and mysterious, a "lone wolf" type. The quiet, shy, odd, or ignored child longs to accomplish something significant and chases the spotlight, longing for accolades. The list goes on.

Are your wheels turning? Does some of what I am saying here ring true? Perhaps you're already recognizing some of the AACTs you've adopted out of your own childhood trauma or impactful events and are carrying around the unfinished business those tender experiences are at the root of.

Ironically, the very AACTs we develop in order to survive can destroy our sense of deep connection to others and to our true self if left unchecked. This disconnect deepens our feelings of not being enough and increases our commitment to our false self until we can no longer distinguish the difference between what's real and what isn't. Or, as Jung puts it, "Loneliness does not come from having no people about one, but from being unable to communicate the things that seem important to oneself, or from holding certain views which others find inadmissible."[10] In the desperate pursuit of belonging, a person will subjugate their real self in the services of the wishes of others without limit. As Jung poignantly states, "The most terrifying thing is to accept oneself completely."[11]

For some, AACTs are experienced as a desperate need to feel significant, coupled with the unbearable condition of feeling ordinary or unseen. This is not to say that no great life is a true life; but it is the case that most people keep the more pained and broken parts of themselves hidden and in the shadows and don't ever bring them into the light—not even for *self*-examination. And often, when they do, it's for attention, acceptance, and, quite frankly, "likes."

This longing for acceptance and approval can force us all into a life that doesn't quite fit us. It may even damage or take away the vibrancy and health that is our birthright.

I see so many beliefs and behaviors that create and sustain a false identity in people and move them into a place and life of misalignment. This then translates into an endless search for purpose, meaning, belonging, and, at times, unreasonable and unhealthy ambition. I have also known numerous people who, having experienced great success in one area, refuse to attempt anything new or risky for fear of failure and its perceived price—loss of the love and adoration they have so desperately strived for and gained. The question I ask is this: Might their lives—our lives, your life—align better if we could all simply be who we were born to be in our purest form? Not who we are trying *to* be or *not* to be for others, but our authentic self? Who might we all become if instead of acceptance and approval we made peace, self-knowing, inner wisdom, and profound purpose our goals?

Belonging and Shame

> *"Shame is a soul-eating emotion."*
> **–CARL GUSTAV JUNG**

Let's address shame (which I see as an acronym for Secrets, Habits, and Acts Mask Embarrassment), which is at the foundation of our AACTs and may even be the biggest contributor to them. AACTs, after all, cover up what we do not want seen, known, or exposed.

Think of a time when you got a letter in the mail for a bill you were unable to pay, or a friend told a group of people something about you that you'd expressly asked them not to mention. You find yourself boiling over, overwhelmed by what I call "hot thoughts." Nothing else can get in your brain, as it is entirely consumed by the inner dialogue that is spinning around and around in your head.

Ding, ding, ding! You have just found telltale signs of shame. Hot thoughts are the "fin above the water" for shame issues.

Let's get this straight: shame and guilt are different. Simply put, guilt is I *did* something wrong, whereas shame is I *am* something wrong.

I *am* something wrong? That's the big one!

Shame exists for a reason, and it goes way back. In *Self-Compassion: Stop Beating Yourself Up and Leave Insecurity Behind*, author Dr. Kristin Neff writes, "Shame was the evolutionary way of us trying to hide our flaws from others. If others knew these flaws, they would kick us out of the group, and evolutionarily that meant death."[12] That's a pretty good incentive to hide parts of yourself, yes?

Much research has been done around belonging and its opposite, "fitting in." Belonging is the full acceptance of who we *truly are*. Fitting in is performing as the "who" we *need to be* in order to fit the space others want us to fill. From early on, we're taught that we won't be accepted unless we AACT like the people who surround us.

Most people associate shame with a traumatic, negative, or humiliating event, but it's often more subtle than that. Shame can come from a number of experiences we share with our parents, educators, friends, and other important authority figures in our lives. Every one of us has experienced it; we were all raised on it, trained by it, and kept in line with it. Let me ask you: Were you ever spanked? Yelled at in front of others? Sent to your room? Teased or left out? Used as "an example"? Those are all moments that almost certainly cause you to feel shame.

After or during the experience of shame and the pain that accompanied it, we learned to hide or fight hard to reflect what we needed to in order to stay in the good graces of others and not be rejected or abandoned—or, as Dr. Neff put it, not to die. Shame often presents as anxiety, evoking sensations like panic and fear. And shame has trained the survivor in us to AACT well—but not honestly.

When I was a little girl, I accidentally killed my goldfish Goldie. I fed her some of my scrambled eggs because I loved her and I wanted to share my bounty with her. When I saw her body float lifelessly to the surface of the bowl, I was terrified. I began to sob uncontrollably.

My family ran in when they heard my sobs. When they saw what I had done, they all broke out in laughter, told me how cute it was, and said they would just get me a new fish.

At that young age, I had no way of communicating the pain I was in. I had just killed something I loved very much. I was scared, and also flush with shame for having done something so stupid—for not knowing better. Though my family's laughter was meant to show support and light-heartedness, it only deepened my feelings of embarrassment and heartbreak.

After their initial humorous outburst, my family lovingly helped me hold a funeral for Goldie. They got me ice cream and a new fish. But the shame from that experience stayed with me. I "AACTed" like I was fine, but I was far from it.

This is one of the early experiences I had that made me a "strong, independent" soldier in the world. Or so it seemed.

I know now that my family members were doing their best and that they were acting out what they had learned and come to hold as truth. They were, in their own way, loving me. But they were also, unwittingly, conditioning me to be inauthentic to my true self.

Reading this, you may not be sure when you have experienced shame. It may help you to know that it presents in many different ways. When it is turned inward, it can create overwhelming feelings of sadness, exhaustion, and loneliness. When it is turned outward, it can express itself as blame, defensiveness, and even anger.

Because we cope with this painful emotion by burying the dark feelings down deep and creating an AACT to mask it, we eventually lose sight of the original self and begin to buy our own bill of goods. Remember what Jung said? A person will subjugate their true self in order to fulfill the wishes of others . . . *without limit*. This subjugation works until it doesn't, and when that happens, life starts to feel wrong, painful, out of alignment. The old tricks stop working and the true self fights to emerge.

This can present itself in several ways. Sometimes you may experience one or all of the emotions mentioned earlier. But other times, as the habitual use of our AACTs breaks down and we can no longer hide behind them, we can start experiencing emotional, spiritual, or energetic blocks, mental fog, anxiety, indecisiveness, depression, addictions, confusion about the future, a midlife crisis, impulsivity, or an overall sense of regret and lack of purpose. Worse yet, we can impose our AACTs on other people. If you've ever told someone to "suck it up" or "just get over it"—or, my favorite, "don't do that, we're in public"—that's an AACT showing up in your words. Many of us tend to work our shame out on others, as it is far easier on us to cause pain rather than feel it.

Years ago, I was at dinner with a friend and some of her friends I'd just met. We were both in town for a conference, and she'd said she wanted us all to meet.

Halfway through the meal, one of the women pulled out a magazine to show us something she'd just referenced in conversation. She flipped to a picture of a well-known actress, dressed in a gorgeous gown.

I opened my mouth to comment on the beauty of the dress—but right as I started talking, my friend squeezed my hand and shushed me.

I stopped speaking mid-sentence. It was awkward.

After dinner, as we walked back to our hotel rooms, I said, "Hey, girl, what was that about?"

Her eyes welled up. "I don't know," she admitted. "It was like I couldn't help myself. I just had this overwhelming feeling of dread."

"Were you afraid of feeling embarrassed about something I might say?"

Tears were streaming down her face now. "I used to feel ashamed of my sister when she would give her opinion about anything because she was loud, caustic, and judgmental like our mother," she blurted out. "Our mother, who drank too much and made everyone uncomfortable."

Shame!

Shame is the original bad guy, and our response to it is shaped by all the emotional memories that surround it (mom, the alcoholic); the deep awareness of how it was experienced previously (my sister embarrassed me); and how we trained ourselves to survive it (shut it down, control it, make it go away). Shame memories are cumulative, as are loss and heartbreak memories, and when a particular emotion is activated in the present moment, they precipitate an instinctive response (grabbing my hand and shushing me). These tiny pockets of emotional memories impact our decisions and reactions, and they can ultimately determine how we govern and live our lives. They can also determine how we impose them on others. As my teacher Tal Ben-Shahar so eloquently states, "Our behavior toward others is often a reflection of our treatment of ourselves."

Lesson 2 Homework: Naming Our AACTs and Taking Responsibility

For this lesson, we'll be breaking our homework up into two separate exercises that will help us get clear about what AACTs we use in order to ensure our belonging in the world, identify the possibilities that are available to us when we rethink our AACTs and take full responsibility for our lives, and distinguish between a "fated" and a "destined" life and understand why that is critical for the creation of our best future self. The second exercise builds on the first, so it's best to do them in order. Together, they will culminate in a full awareness of the ways in which you respond to the world around you to gain approval and acceptance from your family, loved ones, peers, and even strangers.

❋ PART 1: GETTING CLEAR ABOUT YOUR AACTS

> *"Man is least himself when he talks in his own person. Give him a mask and he will tell you the truth."*
>
> **–OSCAR WILDE**

The objective of this exercise is to get a clear and specific picture of the AACTs you use in the world. It is the start of witnessing with compassion the person you present to others versus the person you hold inside, or perhaps the part you have completely lost sight of.

To begin, just sit quietly and think about the most turbulent, challenging, heartbreaking, traumatic, and impactful times you've experienced in your life. Think of yourself during those times; note the evolution of what you were becoming. Trace your entire timeline, from childhood up until today.

Now ask yourself these questions and, tracking what comes into your awareness as you do, take notes on your responses:

- How have I shown up in the world to make people accept me when I'm going through something painful?
- Who have I become for my family? Friends? Romantic partners? Communities?
- What do I do to get attention, affection, or love?
- What feedback have I been looking for from those around me, and what feedback have I gotten? Do I like it?
- How has this feedback solidified my AACTs?
- How do my AACTs contribute to the way I see myself and others?
- How do they support my beliefs and mantras?
- How do I want the world to see me, regardless of the cost?
- What voice do I feel stirring deep down, and what is it trying to say?
- What is my most prominent AACT, and how did it shape my behavior and identity in my life?
- When you focus on this new awareness, what do you sense is missing on a deeper level?
- Who might you be without it/them?

Hopefully, a clear picture of the masks you wear in the world, as well as an understanding of how they no longer serve you and the possibility that what you have been hiding is of great value to both you and the world around you, is beginning to take shape for you.

Now let's connect the dots between what you learned as a child and the person those lessons have molded you into. Think about heartbreaks in your life and what you did afterward to be certain everybody accepted you and thought well of you—or at the very least paid attention to you. Did you do extra well in school? Did you try to impress others? Did you become a leader? Did you become shy or withdrawn, or simply keep to yourself? Did you become the troubled, hardened teen—the negative attention getter? Maybe you started using makeup or became the perfect, popular student. Perhaps you excelled at sports and became a great competitor. Or did you become the dependable caregiver for others—the indispensable, take-control, reliable one in your friend group or family?

Take a moment to review the "Tilling the Soil" writing exercise from Chapter 6 and your MMB (Models, Mantras, and Beliefs) exercise from your Chapter 7 assignment.

After you review both, try to distinguish which impactful events or MMBs have contributed to the development of your AACTs. Once you've identified those, ask yourself, *What behaviors do I continue to carry with me in the world today?* For example, when I started struggling in my high school math class (because, as I noted earlier, I was and am very dyslexic with numbers), I began to excel at dance, art, law, and creative writing. I also became very social, more popular, and a bit of a fashionista. (It's no wonder that I became a professional dancer, actor, singer, writer, and creative entrepreneur, right?) So many of our AACTs become baked in; in fact, they become *so* normal to us that we eventually struggle to distinguish between what is real and what's an AACT—we think of them not as our second nature but as our *actual* nature.

Once you review your writing exercise and MMBs, write down at least five AACTs you can clearly see as being part of the face you present to the world. Next, think of some of the things those AACTs have led you to say to people. Now, take it a step further: write down some AACTs you've seen in others, think how knowing that their actions were prompted by their AACTs at the time might have changed how you responded in the moment, and imagine what you might be able to let go of in the future now that you have this new awareness.

Now, since we also tend to impose these AACTs on others—expecting others to act in the world as we do, even expressing our inner voices as an adviser or controller—ask yourself, *What are some of the responses to the outer world my AACTs create?*

Use the chart provided here (download and print at www.unfinishedbusiness/worksheets, or sketch out your own version on a piece of paper) to initiate your homework. Again, please review both your "Tilling the Soil" and MMBs homework. Distinguish which impactful events or MMBs you have turned into AACTs. Notice if those events have caused your AACTs to change and cumulatively grow over time. Take note of any escalation in behaviors as you've moved through each life event. Continue to assess which behaviors you continue to carry with you in the present.

ACCEPTANCE AND APPROVAL CREATES TRICKS (AACT):
What you do to cope and to be accepted by the outside world?

EXAMPLE: TAMMY

MMB:

(Mo) (father) Follow the traditional path to make it in this world. Men are sensible women are not. Learn to work hard and always be likeable. (Mother) Women are quite and well behaved. Do as you are told. Get married and be a good wife.

(MA) "Art is a hobby not a dream to follow." "You are not good enough or smart enough to follow your dreams." "You are like a child." "Get a real job." "Find a man to support you." "Don't make waves."

(B) It's childish to stay true to your heart. Only good girls to get love. Women are powerless without a hardworking man. Keep your crazy bohemian ideas to yourself. Life is hard so play it safe. Learn to fit in.

AACT'S: Tammy presented to the world as obedient. A good girl. Nice. Perhaps a Martyr or Saint. She was agreeable so as not to offend or lose love. shy and coy at times.
To gain approval at school she became the teacher's pet looking for acceptance and accolades. She worked lunch hours in the principal's office for extra credit so her father would think she was a high achiever. She became overly focused on looking pretty, always put together and attractive.

RESPONSE: "I know life can be difficult at times but don't complain." "Always do your best." "Don't make trouble or you'll get fired. Do your work." "I love being creative too but it's risky. Make it your hobby."

MMB: _____

AACT'S: _____

RESPONSE: _____

MMB: _____

AACT'S: _____

RESPONSE: _____

MMB: _____

AACT'S: _____

RESPONSE: _____

MMB: _____

AACT'S: _____

RESPONSE: _____

❋ PART 2: THE FATED AND DESTINED LIVES

"That's right, Five, always put the blame on others."
–LEWIS CARROLL

In our early life, our experiences and the way we react to them are often dictated to us by our authority figures, teachers, friends, and communities. As we become adults, we must learn how to design, plant, and tend to our own garden—in other words, we must take full ownership and responsibility for our life and the way we show up for it, give it care, react to it, and shape its future growth.

In moving through this next section, you will begin to understand that destiny is active and fate is passive. Whereas destiny is a choice (or series of choices), fate is the lack thereof; it is essentially the belief that we are victims of the weeds that have grown beyond our control—weeds that, because we didn't plant them, we think aren't our responsibility to deal with. It's also the lack of understanding that if we just make the commitment to tend to our life's garden—to both pull weeds and plant seeds—we can create a destiny filled with beauty and healthy abundance. Surrendering to a lack of agency is how we begin to experience overwhelming feelings—aka weed overgrowth—and, ultimately, how we lose sight of what we are here to manifest and celebrate. It blinds us to the fact that we are all here to plant seeds of purpose, abundance, joy, and love for ourselves.

What does taking full responsibility for our lives really look like, no matter what the circumstances?

A client of mine, Cathy, was married with seven children. She had left her career as an executive to be a stay-at-home mom and wife. She loved it. Then, just when the last of her kids had finally entered preschool, her husband fell in love with another woman—a woman who was quite a bit younger than Cathy. ("He couldn't have fallen in love with her at kid number two—he had to wait until number seven?" she joked to me in one of our sessions.) He left the family and Cathy was left to deal with the fallout, including the finances, all on her own. Her former career was no longer an option.

When I started to work with her, Cathy was beyond brokenhearted. She was also very scared. And it would have been easy for her to embrace the role of "victim" in this situation. She could have ruminated upon the fact that her husband betrayed her; she could have believed in the narrative that he'd "ruined her life." But once she truly started to see life from the perspective of self-responsibility, she didn't! Instead of dwelling on what her husband had done, she began designing her future. She did the work to heal her heart and then started her own business helping women who'd found themselves in similar situations. She even managed to become friendly with her ex-husband so they could coparent their many children.

Like Cathy, most of us are blindsided when heartbreak happens to us; but regardless of the circumstance, we *all* have a choice of whether to respond or to react. *Reacting* involves blame (remember, blame is shame turned outward): we try to make ourselves right and someone else wrong— we choose the "fated" life. The fated life tells the story of someone who refuses responsibility and in doing so loses the chance at a better outcome. Or, as Jung put it, "When an inner situation is not made conscious, it appears outside as fate." We become the victim. In Cathy's case, this would have entailed blaming the dissolution of her marriage totally on her husband and refusing to do the emotional work required in order to forgive the past and embrace her future. As a result, she would have stayed bitter and stuck—incapable of moving toward a fresh start.

Responding like Cathy did, in contrast, requires taking a step back to consider what happened, how that situation came to be, and the ways in which we may be contributing to the situation or the solution through our own choices. It requires us to rise above our circumstances, objectively view our entire garden, determine which plants are nourishing and securing our topsoil and which are choking out new growth, and then methodically nurturing the former and removing the latter.

When we choose to see people and situations how they *are*, not how we *wish* they were, we propel ourselves out of the victim mindset and into a new realm of possibility. In my experience as a coach, I have found that people who not only accept what is real but also are willing to find the lessons and blessings in the most challenging of times exhibit higher levels of resilience, happiness, health, and success. This is what I call living a *destined* life.

The destined life is one defined by choice, awareness, action, forgiveness, and gratitude. It is a garden built by design. Destiny has direction and requires action on the part of the person involved. Even if you think of it as a path already laid out for you, you still must walk it. In order to follow the path that leads to our highest potential and most meaningful future, we have to take massive and positive action—as well as responsibility for absolutely everything that appears in our life, the good *and* the difficult. This act alone is the choice of the victor!

What are the areas of life in which you want to take charge of your destiny, and what actions do you need to take in order to move in that direction? Using the chart provided (download and print at www.unfinishedbusiness/ worksheets, or sketch out your own version on a piece of paper), make a list of events, large or small, and tell the story of each one as someone who refuses responsibility and loses control over creating a better outcome in the fated life areas.

Now rewrite the script in the destined life areas: Depict the situations as how they *truly are*, not how you *wish* they were. Free yourself of the victim mindset so that you can see the possibilities in the circumstances—the flowers among the weeds—and the many choices and creative opportunities each one offers.

An example might be:

THE FATED LIFE: My ex left me for another woman, and now I'm raising our children by myself. He's a horrible person, and I hate him for leaving me stuck holding the bag for the rest of my life. I'll never survive. Why would God do this to me?

Now try reframing it into:

THE DESTINED LIFE: My ex left me. I wasn't thriving in that relationship, and now I have the capacity to build the next powerful and passionate chapter of my life. I will do the work I need to do to heal and I will raise our children in a loving environment, free from the difficulties and tensions our relationship created. I am free to pursue my own passions and dreams. I am about to find out what I am capable of and how much courage I have. When I choose to, I will find a new partner—one who deeply loves me—and together we will co-create the life of our dreams. I am strong and capable. I am determined to build the greatest life possible for myself and my children. I have the rest of my life to look forward to, and I am excited about all the new opportunities and growth I am about to embark upon—I may even start my own business!

THE FATED LIFE	THE DESTINED LIFE
1.	1.
2.	2.
3.	3.
4.	4.
5.	5.

In this lifetime, heartbreak is not optional—and if left unresolved, it will build a wall around our hearts that we cannot climb over on our own. So, instead of trying to run from it, we must learn to recover from it and find meaning in it. The work we're doing here is a skill that will keep your heart open and give you the ability to respond—not react—to life.

Can you imagine being able to choose your relationship to the heartbreaks, disappointments, and unwanted changes in your life? Can you imagine being able to stay present the next time you experience a deeply challenging or painful situation and not lose control or be hijacked by your emotions? Can you imagine no longer creating messes that need to be cleaned up later? Are you starting to envision a life of responsibility and not reactivity? *Bravo!*

Critical Notes Before You Do Your Homework for This Chapter

One of the primary thoughts I want to get you to deeply understand with this work is this: unfinished business—past traumas of any kind, big or small—cannot be healed, solved, or completed in the brain (there's a reason we don't call ourselves "mindbroken" or "brain-crushed" when something painful happens to us!). There is no way to "think" your way out of heartbreak. Our losses, changes, transitions, and traumas are energetically stored in our *bodies*. That's why finding them and releasing them is at the core of the work we are doing in this course. Heartbreak is a feeling experience, not a thinking experience—so the work we will be moving through together will be executed in the energetic and emotional body . . . not in the head or mind.

The only way the heart can truly be healed is if you literally move the energetic memories that are no longer necessary to you out of your body at a cellular level. You have got to release the truth—all of it. The catch? The body will not release the old story unless it knows that your understanding of it is whole, honest, and complete. The body and the universe keep a perfect set of books. Therefore, *truth*—at its deepest level—is critical.

Magical or wishful thinking or *spiritual bypassing* (which we will talk about soon) does not help with healing trauma or an incomplete past; nor does ignoring it and hoping it will go away in time. Dealing with the pain of heartbreak and loss in the mind may soothe it in the moment—it may pacify the energy at first—but the only way to truly recover from your wounds is to take real action and uproot it from the body to make space for new love, new light, and a fresh life to take root and blossom.

Homework Follow-Up

Now that you've reviewed all of your AACTs and committed to taking full responsibility for yourself and your life, and now that you have a deeper understanding of what creating a destined life versus a fated one looks like, let's imagine how you can take this fresh information out into the world around you. I want you to take a moment to review how you've AACT-ed in the world to *externally* cope. Look at the language you use when you speak to yourself and others. Then review your destiny versus fate chart and view them all like a tapestry—one in which every thread of data weaves together to form an image of who you have been in the world. Let your new awareness of this version of yourself become your friend on your journey.

> *"What we call the personality is often a jumble of genuine traits and adopted coping styles that do not reflect our true self at all but the loss of it."*
>
> **–GABOR MATÉ**

Spend the next few days being fully conscious of the AACTs you use; flag for yourself when you're turning on an AACT instead of dealing openly and honestly with your own or others' feelings. Notice where you avoid responsibility. Notice choices you make or stories you tell that keep you in the fated column and away from the open field of destiny, and steer yourself away from them. To start with, it is enough to simply shed light on these AACTs and avoidance techniques you have been using for most of your life. To name them and to claim them is half the battle.

Keep in mind that this is a lifelong practice, and the more you do it the more honed your skills will become. I don't expect you to notice every single AACT or avoidance technique in your arsenal at this point; I just want you to start paying attention to when and where these behaviors arise in your life, why they show up, and what it is you truly want.

Here are four questions to carry with you and ask yourself when an AACT has just come to call:

1. Which AACT was that?
2. What triggered it?
3. What body sensations occurred before, during, and after?
4. What did I *really* want in that moment?

Higher Self-Talk

I'm aware of my deep desire for belonging and I know I am not alone in this. Everyone has experienced the pain brought on by shame at one time or another. I thought I needed to AACT a certain way to belong to my community, to the people I wanted near, to the people I love, to the world I needed validation from. I understand now that I am more than my AACTs. I am more than someone who is fated to behave a certain way and simply react to life from a place of fear. Shame and the need to belong kept me in a place that protected me for a long time, but I am now ready to respond to life intentionally—to own the fact that I have a choice about how I show up as myself, relate to others, and behave when life isn't seeming to go my way or the unexpected happens. I am ready and prepared to listen to my true voice. I am so grateful for this fresh understanding that I am enough. I no longer need pretense or personas. I no longer need the mask of perfection and control. I am proud of the work I've done—and I feel ready to step into my life with full authenticity, transparency, and vulnerability. And *that* is no AACT.

Chapter 9:
Lesson 3

I loved soft pretzels! I lived for them! If I was stressed, pretzels. If I felt happy, pretzels. Since I was a kid, pretzels. I could spend two hours a day looking for the best soft pretzels or revisiting my favorites. Until I put on an extra eighty pounds.

When that happened, I went into a depression—and then I went in search of a weight loss program. Oh boy! Nothing worked. I started to realize that eating pretzels was more of an emotional compulsion than a dietary choice. Then I came across and attended an open class about Unfinished Business, and something just clicked.

Investigating and understanding the heartbreaks and disappointments of my past, of my childhood, and how my mother and father would pacify me with food brought me to tears—and believe me, I am not a crier. Even the normal dysfunction of childhood can break a kid's heart.

There was a great deal of neglect and verbal abuse in my childhood but my parents did the best they could, I suppose. They did not have a great marriage, they were not communicators, and they handled everything with distractions, of which food was the biggest and pretzels were numero uno!

I spent about a year digging deep into my unfinished business. I became very aware of my energy, my charge, and my coping mechanisms. As I cleared the energy of the past, my cravings literally subsided. Completely! I not only lost the eighty pounds, but with the extra time I had on my hands (because I was no longer perpetually in search of the perfect carb), I became a Reiki master. That was something I'd always dreamed of as a side gig to being a solid businessman. Now I help people daily.

I know myself so much better now. I have deeper relationships. I choose differently and I have the courage and desire to pursue things I only dreamed about in the past. I still really love pretzels, but I only eat them when I choose to, not when I feel a deep unexamined need to.

–CHUCK

"Everybody's talking about Energy Psychology these days. We seem to have finally figured out that the mind alone does not heal, and that the body is an essential component of mental health. Energy is the interface between mind and body. Just as the electricity in your computer allows the hardware and software to interface, the life force that runs through you connects your body and mind. That life force is known by many names: Yogis call it prana; Oriental medicine calls it qi or chi; the Star Wars movies called it 'the Force.' Bioenergetics is the study of the human personality in terms of the energetic processes of the body. In bioenergetic therapy, we call this energy 'charge.'"

–ANODEA JUDITH

I sucked my thumb until I was a teenager. I did. It calmed me. As a seriously ill child, going in and out of hospitals and doctors' offices for eleven years of my life was a tough reality. I carried a lot of stress and anxiety in my body, and having a "binky" attached to my hand was a saving grace. When I went to an unfamiliar hospital or doctor's office, sucking my thumb gave me the courage to show up as a well-behaved little girl who could handle the prodding and probing one goes through in those circumstances.

As I got older, before every stress-inducing test I took in school, I would go to the school lavatory, sit in the stall, and suck my thumb for a few minutes. It worked to calm my nerves and keep scary emotions at bay. It refocused my energy, gave me a feeling of agency. My thumb was what stopped me from falling apart in times of inner terror. It put me to sleep every night. It quieted the anxiety that is brought on by early trauma and experiences of the unknown. It gave me back some modicum of control. It changed the vibrant yet agitated current of energy that was coursing through my body from unmanageable to manageable. It made me feel safer.

My illness and surgery changed me—made me a hypervigilant child and caused me to have intense reactions to the stressors in my world. My mother told me that, post-surgery, every time I saw bright lights or a white coat—both reminiscent of an operating room and the doctors in it—my body would get tense, I would start to panic, and I would fight to catch my breath. It could take hours to calm me down.

Through the years, panic would be my response to many scary or stressful circumstances in my life.

For many years, I wondered why I had such a visceral response to these things. Now I know that back in the days of my surgery, doctors used ether rather than anesthesia on children. Whereas anesthesia, when done right, blocks pain completely (and sends you in a sleeplike state), ether provokes a choking, suffocating response: it paralyzes you, but you still feel pain. Can you imagine the trapped energy I must have been holding in my body after being tied down to an operating table and having surgery performed on me—unable to move, respond, or protect myself despite the pain I was in? Can you also imagine how desperately my body wanted to complete and release that powerful, traumatized energy? (And this on top of the eleven months of illness prior to the surgery, and the isolation and loneliness I experienced afterward when I was left alone in the hospital to recover.)

It's no surprise, then, that I held an inner sense of terror all my life until I discovered what was at the root of it. Until that discovery, my thumb was the glue that held me together. That little thumb stopped that powerful, trapped charge from wreaking havoc; it held it at bay, held it in place. It allowed me to show up in the world the way people expected me to. However, it also blocked the path of that energy and did not allow me to release its surge the way my body needed me to.

This lesson is all about the emotional energy we store in our body, the pacifying behaviors we use to calm, stop, freeze, or re-freeze our experiences and sensations of pain, anxiety, and overwhelm, and how releasing that pent-up energy can bring us back to a blessedly neutral place—back into the present moment, where our life is *actually* occurring. It is a deep dig into the depth of your behaviors and what they really mean—an exploration into the way you operate on a deeper, unconscious level. Be prepared: this lesson is a powerful one, and a long one.

Typically, when mining for something, you look for changes that appear at the surface—indicators that hint at what lies beneath, subtle signs that beg for deeper exploration. In this lesson, we will be looking at the surface habits, reactions, coping behaviors, and numbing techniques that keep us away from the deep, scary, buried—and at times paralyzing—feelings of our distant and recent past.

We will also discuss what *charge* is, and examine how what I call our *charge changers* impact our productivity, follow-through, success, relationships, self-awareness, and clarity in life. We will discover how the energy that is still trapped in our bodies travels and rises to the surface, causing active *charge*, and what we grasp for when it does. We will develop an understanding around how these elevated sensations cause us to do whatever we can to adjust and avoid discomfort.

In this lesson, we're looking for the things we do to deaden those unnerving sensations in order to cope, survive, and behave in an acceptable way. We're looking for our thumbs and binkies so we can unearth the trapped charge that is hidden beneath them—and release it once and for all.

What Is Charge?

Charge is quite literally our aliveness—the life force that runs through our body. It has been called lots of things—chi, prana, libido, and more. When it's in balance, charge is good, healthy, essential, and incredibly helpful. It is what makes us feel our emotions, sensations, and inner experiences. It is the power behind motivation and ambition. It is the source of attraction, passion, purpose, and drive. It is the juice that heats our engine and cools our jets. Charge gives life meaning; without it, we would become mechanical beings.

The ability to manage charge is at the foundation of a joyful and successful life. To be truly healthy and happy, we need a free and balanced flow of this energy throughout our bodies. We need to be able to call on it when we need to and quiet it when it has run amok.

Most importantly, we need our charge to be healthy and robust so we can use it to accomplish our dreams and build loving, authentic relationships. It is the source of connection—and the magic of being human.

What Is Incomplete Charge?

When we speak of incomplete charge in this book, we are referring to the thwarted survival energy that gets trapped in the body as the result of an incomplete self-protective motor response. This happens in reaction to both acute and cumulative stressors that overwhelm our natural defensive responses, injuring our autonomic nervous system and its ability to self-regulate.

Dr. Peter A. Levine, a PhD in both medical biophysics (University of California, Berkeley) and psychology (International University), a pioneer in the field of bioenergetics, somatic healing, and the study of trauma, and the author of *Waking the Tiger*, explains it this way: "When we feel that our lives are threatened, our bodies naturally charge up for fight or flight. If neither of those two options are available, we fall back to the third option, to freeze—to trick a predator into thinking we're dead and giving us a potential opportunity for escape later . . . once it is safe, an animal will eventually shake and tremble, discharging all that fight or flight energy. However, in trauma, we stay stuck in freeze, either there is too much, too soon, or too little, too long, and the animal (i.e., us) isn't able to process, discharge and integrate the experience."[13]

Levine became interested in studying the effect stress has on animals' nervous systems when it occurred to him that wild animals are consistently under the threat of death and yet never show signs of trauma. In his studies, he discovered that trauma has to do with our third survival response to danger, overwhelm, or stress, which is to simply *freeze*. When our fight or flight responses are not accessible to us—as was true for me when I was on the operating table—we literally freeze and immobilize. Animals sometimes freeze or play dead—but once the danger has passed, they release their frozen energy through physical movement: trembling, shaking, and so on. If that huge amount of fight or flight energy that the body has "charged up" in order to protect us does not get discharged or released, however, the charge stays trapped and the body continues to believe it is under threat.

Let's unpack this a bit more. Charge, the physical and energetic response to significant experiences, thoughts, memories, and relationships, is an amazing system set up by nature in order to give us awareness and make us feel alive. However, what we block, hold in, hold back, and hold onto does not just vaporize into thin air. These feelings and this energy live in our bodies, just waiting for triggers to charge us up the next time we encounter a situation, memory, or person that provokes a similar response.

Almost everyone has (or has seen) a closet or basement cluttered with stuff. Some items in storage remain useful if organized and deemed important, but most of what we keep is old and unnecessary—perhaps even unusable. But for many of us, it's difficult to go through that storage and throw things away because we have emotions and memories tied to each object. Say, for instance, that you're cleaning out the basement and find an old board game. Feelings arise in your stomach, heart, and/or throat (this is stored, unresolved, and incomplete business that is locked away in your body as *charge* showing up!), and you think something like, *OMG . . . I remember when I used to play this with my dad. I miss him so much; wish I had been able to say goodbye. I can't get rid of this game; it reminds me too much of him.*

This is an understandable response—but is it serving you?

Every one of us has experienced charge—you know, those feelings of excitement, fear, agitation, thrill, joy, or even sexual arousal that make our lives worth living. Blocked or imbalanced charge, however, can create real issues—and once our body is full of it, we stop being able to feel and react to life's circumstances with a neutral (i.e., *accurate*) barometer.

When I was on QVC as a product spokesperson, we had to train with and be approved by the channel before going on the air. We spent a full day learning how to sell and present the products, how to use our hands on the products, and so on. On my training day, a dynamic entrepreneur who had a brilliant line of home products was one of the vendors participating. He was a blast—fun energy, great sense of humor, smart, and well spoken. But when it was his turn to test on camera and talk about his product, he froze—and I mean literally. There was a complete halting of his energy. We talked afterward, and I learned that he'd held terror around making a mistake or failing since childhood.

This is a perfect example of how imbalanced charge can stop us from taking action in our lives and damage our chances at success (not to mention ruin our relationships, our attitude, and our everyday experiences). When we are undercharged, we can suffer from depression and lethargy, and become disinterested in our world. We can also miss great opportunities to make our deepest dreams come true.

In this lesson we will be working to identify this repressed, frozen energy so we can recharge it and then discharge it. You'll begin to observe and identify your *charge changers*—the coping behaviors and mechanisms everyone uses to keep difficult emotions at bay, and that we get so good at that we think, *This is just the way I am.* The truth, however, is that it's just the way you *learned* to be in order to hold yourself together at some point in your life.

These techniques are clever—but they're holding you back. So it's time to shine a light on them and learn to let them go.

How Charge Shows Up

Have you ever fallen in love? Or had to tell someone you've fallen out of it? Have you ever had a powerful reaction to a dramatic scene in a movie? Have you ever lost someone and felt your body collapse at the news? Have you ever panicked and felt paralyzed when walking into a big moment in your life? Take a moment to think about how your body felt during times like these—the sensations in your belly, the tingling of your face and hands, the racing of your heart, the deepening of your breath, the sting in your eyes, the rise in body temperature, or the deep need to squirm or move as you attempted to process something exciting, unexpected, or powerful. This is active charge.

When you experience charge that is attached to more painful emotions, your body may experience a form of energetic choking: You may tense up or stop breathing deeply; your throat may close up; your chest may feel tight and your stomach may turn to stone. You may experience chills or sweats and your shoulders and neck may feel locked or tense. Your whole body may feel flushed with heat. You may even shake or forget how to swallow. The degree of emotion establishes the degree of charge, and the type of emotion can establish the direction of the charge. For example, anger will typically move outward, while sadness will typically move inward.

When charge is intellectualized, it can lead to great creativity and inspiration. It can also be the fuel behind the inner critic that loops in your brain or the constant worry that keeps you up at night even though there is no real threat in sight.

It's important to remember that, at its core, charge is neutral. It's our experience and perception of it, and the unfinished business that surrounds it, that determines how it flows through us—as a positive or negative experience. Examined and directed charge leads to examined and directed life force.

Take a moment here to think about something that upsets you. It does not have to be a huge issue in your life right now, just something that makes you squirm a little. Notice the sensations, simple and complex, happening in your body as you think about this thing. Check yourself from the Root Brain, through the REAL Brain, and all the way up to the Royal Brain. Get quiet. What do you notice? Any sensations? Any movement? If so, where? In your belly or heart? Your throat or hands? Are you experiencing any tension anywhere? Any words or judgmental thoughts? Notice.

This is active charge. And whatever you feel compelled to do to stop those sensations—move around, change your thoughts, check your email, make a joke, get mad, judge yourself and others, criticize the process, start to cry—these are *charge changers*.

Why Charge Matters

Can you imagine going through life without the sensation of charge? If everything felt the same? If nothing required you to move fast, laugh hard, express passion, or cry out with joy or sorrow? As much as we may complain about pain or our darker emotions, think about the alternative: nothingness. Not so appealing, right?

Energy is what animates us and the world around us. The free flow of that energy allows us to live a vibrant, exuberant life. The blockage of that energy diminishes our experience of the world and of ourselves.

Now, can you imagine a life free of *blocked* charge? A life in which you are no longer reactive to highly triggering situations in your life?

Charge is controlled by our programming. This is how one of my teachers, Anodea Judith, explains it in her book *Charge and the Energy Body* (bracketed additions mine!): "Onto your hardware [*the physical body*], enormous amounts of software have been installed—all your conscious and unconscious programming [*what I call models, mantras, and beliefs*]. From the basic instincts that are 'hardwired' into your body, to the memories, beliefs, and learning that you have accumulated over a lifetime, including the language you speak and the habits you've developed, this software is stored on your hardware, in the muscles, nerve pathways, and central processing unit of the brain. It may include the innate knowledge of how to ride a bicycle, play a piece on the piano, or speak a foreign language. Your software also includes your self-concept, your worldview, your religious beliefs, and the thoughts that guide your actions. Much of this programming was installed before you were old enough to notice it—basically from the day you were born, if not earlier. . . . Most of us are unconsciously run by our programming. None of us escape having it."[14]

Your models, mantras, beliefs, and behaviors—those are your programming. And your programming is what tells your life force where to go and where not to go. That is why getting to the bottom of your programming is essential to understanding your relationship to charge and to yourself.

Have you ever known anyone who refuses to cry or delve in any way into their inner well of expression and emotion? You may have heard them say something like, "Don't make me cry," or "I promised myself I wouldn't cry." This desire not to feel too deeply can be brought on by early modeling, societal beliefs and pressures, or shame experiences. Alexander Lowen, MD, has this to say in his book *The Voice of The Body*: "As adults, we have many inhibitions against crying. We feel it is an expression of weakness, or femininity or of childishness. The person who is afraid to cry is afraid of pleasure."[15] Can you recognize the person he's referring to here? Can you see their MMBs and the blocked charge they are likely carrying?

As human beings, we tend to push our more challenging emotions down—primarily because of our beliefs about fully expressing them—which in turn blocks our charge and freezes our energy. Dr. Levine hypothesizes that humans cannot effortlessly release energy from a painful, devastating, heartbreaking, or traumatic experience or memory because of our triune (three-part) brain structure—not to be confused with the three brains we discussed earlier; those are different!—which, shaped by feelings and acumen, frequently supersedes instinct. In other words, because of our ability to think, reason, and *bypass*, we stop ourselves from completing our own emotional jarring.

Learning to control our charge, to charge ourselves when needed, and to discharge what is no longer serving us is at the center of emotional and physiological health. Dr. Levine calls this process learning to "renegotiate" rather than "reenact" the charge (the latter of which so many of us do unwittingly, responding the same way over and over when faced with events that trigger our unfinished business).

If we want to break the cycle, we need to understand where the charge lies. One of the best ways to do that is to get comfortable noticing when we feel charge in our bodies and to create an awareness around our *charge-changing* behaviors.

Charge Changers vs. Charge Choices

Let's take a good look at what charge changers—those coping mechanisms we developed so long ago—can look like.

Our internalized energetic experiences of loss, heartbreak, change, and trauma—all our unfinished business—come up into our conscious mind and body again and again because these body memories are taking up space and need our attention. This is scary for us, because we don't want any of the attached hurt, pain, and sorrow to emerge with them. They, however, very much want to surface. They need us to help them.

Have you ever heard someone say, "Why do I keep attracting the same [insert word here: men, women, situations, disappointments, etc.]?" These recurring situations in our lives are our subconscious mind and our unfinished business telling us that there is something going on under the surface trying to be heard and healed. Old, unresolved issues of the past stay on a loop in our lives until we hear them and clear them. As long as we do not do that, they will continue showing up and pointing their finger at where we are blocked; they will bring us circumstance after circumstance that will push us to take our unfinished business seriously and deal with it head-on; they will continue urging us to examine the things we don't want to resurface because we fear the discomfort doing so will cause.

Therein lies the struggle, because we have designed tricks and traps that try to block their way. We want them to stay quiet and hidden—down in the caverns of our being, deep beneath the soil of our gardens. Our habit is to fill our lives, our spaces, and our time with distractions so we don't have to think about this energy, or to bury it in a place that doesn't make us feel so uneasy. Then we look for our "thumb" or our "binky"—or, like Chuck, our food—to calm the anxiety or pain when it tries to resurface. Whenever we have quiet moments and the stored energy sneaks back into our consciousness—usually in the form of memories or painful feelings—we rush to occupy, distract, or soothe ourselves somehow.

Have you ever had a bad day and found yourself at Home Depot or Target, just shopping away? That's you being overcharged. Or, the opposite—you woke up feeling blue and just decided to play hooky and watch reruns of *The Bachelor* all day? That's you being undercharged.

Often, we get so good at these distractions that we lose our awareness around what is neutral and natural behavior and what is charge changing. To avoid feelings of overwhelm or even inadequacy, we distract and entertain ourselves with television and other media. To avoid our inner ache, we might call a friend and talk for hours, read a book, work or overwork, go to the gym, or buy a few things online. We may eat something, drink something, or try to control someone else. Sometimes we do more elaborate things like dress up and go out somewhere or do something that makes us feel important or significant. These distractions become such second nature that we don't even realize that the past is in the driver's seat and has taken hold of our future.

Many of the behaviors we use to address charge are very normal everyday activities we would not survive (or at least thrive) without. Imagine not eating food or hanging out with friends—not much of a life! The point here, however, is not *when* or *that* we do them but *why* we do them. These are the little red flags in our minefield. If you feel charge or notice yourself moving into your charge changers, you have found a flag, and then you know you're on to something beneath the surface—in fact, you're about to step right in it. *Kaboom!*

If we can examine what our charge changers look like, find the frozen charge that lies beneath, and then learn to change those reactive behaviors into *charge choices*—conscious choices we make from a healed, healthy, and neutral place—the whole game shifts and we find ourselves able to take control of the direction of our lives. As we answer the call of our past experiences and clear the emotional baggage we've been carrying around, we free ourselves up for a fresh way of being—a new way of living.

How Charge Starts Getting Blocked

When my son, Gideon, was in the third grade his teacher called me in because she was frustrated by the fact that he liked to stand at his desk during class, particularly during tests.

"It's distracting the other students," she said. "I'd like you to talk to Gideon and let him know that he should sit at all times in class, unless told otherwise."

Hmmm, I thought, and I stayed quiet for a moment to gather my thoughts. After a beat I asked, "Does he have comprehension issues with the material?"

"No," she admitted.

"Does standing prevent him from contributing to the class or completing his work?" I pressed.

"No," she said slowly. "Overall, Gideon is a joy to have in class and his classmates love him. But," she insisted, "I really need him to sit still!"

I did talk to Gideon, but not to tell him to sit still. Instead, I asked him why he was standing during class.

"Sitting still in my seat is too hard, Mama," he explained while kicking his chair and pushing his matchbox car around the table. "If I have to sit, I can't think about anything else. All I think about is not moving and it makes me want to move more!"

A smile crossed my face. "Do you like school?"

He answered with such enthusiasm it made me laugh. "I love school! I really like to learn, and standing helps me learn better. Why can't everybody just stand?"

I have to say, there is no one I love talking to more than Gideon—even to this day!

A few days later, I met for a second time with Gideon's teacher, a lovely woman, and I explained that the answer was not in making him sit—aka *blocking* his energy flow or charge—but rather changing his seat so he would not disturb the other students while he was functioning the way he was wired to. He needed to be given the space to experience his necessary flow of energy, the charge he *needed* in order to function at his highest capacity. Luckily, she heard me, and together we came up with a way for my son to be himself entirely while protecting the other kids from disruption. My son became an exceptional student, and with maturity, he was eventually able to manage his own charge and energy.

How many of us were able to behave in school, to sit still and be quiet, all the while forcing our inner charge to shut up and shut down? As a society, we tend to punish charge in children, shame them to get them to obey, and pressure them from a place of our own unresolved shame and charge to fit in and be "normal." At times they are even bribed into this kind of "good" behavior. Do you remember being offered a gold star, a piece of candy, or some other reward if you would "just sit still"? This teaches children to hold in their charge—locking it into their bodies—and also begins the process of feeling shame around it. Because of this constant suppression and repression, our experiences of joy, emotional freedom, aliveness, and self-agency diminish over time.

In overriding and containing urges and charge in a misguided attempt to "normalize," we become "*self*-conscious" and lose our ability to hear our own inner voice and intuition. We lose the ability to direct and manage our energy. This is when and how we learn to stop asking for what we truly want in life.

The Hunt for Charge Changers

First, we need to see what we do when we try to either control or hide from our triggered charge—i.e., when we turn to our *charge changers*. Once we discover what these pacifying behaviors and coping mechanisms are, where they began, and where and when they show up in our lives, we will examine what lies beneath and then go in for the big cleanup.

In order to attain clarity around what our harmful behaviors are, where they came from, who they belong to, and what thoughts keep us attached to them, we must learn to *stop pushing our broken hearts out of the way in search of temporary relief and control*. We desperately need to start using our bodies, our three brains, and our spirits as well-oiled processing machines rather than as storage units for our blocked energy and pain.

The first step to this part of the process is to learn what our charge and charge changers look like, what triggers them, what we are avoiding by using them, and where they were born. We cannot simply change the way we think about them; we must find where they are stored, bring them out and shine a light on them, name them, recharge them, and then release them completely in order to bring our system back to a place of neutrality.

When I work with clients on difficult issues, I'm always on the lookout for charge—especially charge they are not even aware of—as it arises. In one notable session, a client was discussing the end of his marriage with what seemed like great ease. He was cool as a cucumber—calm and collected. When we got on the topic of his ex-wife remarrying (trigger), his face didn't change expression, but I noticed some subtle clues that his charge was on the rise: his ears got bright red and his fingers started to fidget and tap. When we dug deeper into that moment, he had a surge of emotion. At first he was angry (overcharged), but that soon gave way to deep sorrow and then exhaustion (discharged), and then back to neutral. When we investigated further, we discovered that whenever he thought about these things he would typically go out for a drink, go to the gym, or go on a date. Those were his charge changers.

The process of allowing ourselves to feel what we've been avoiding may be uncomfortable, but unlocking the barriers between what we need to heal and what we are afraid to feel is key to this work—and the payoff is worth far more than the price of admission. If we can learn not to fear our feelings of heartbreak or sorrow, we can begin to free ourselves from their grip. We can learn to embrace our painful experiences and transform them into opportunities for deep change, self-knowledge, and profound growth. Throughout this process, stories and memories of pain will arise—there is no way to avoid this part of the work—but following those upwellings, the fear and anger we've stored inside will finally discharge and clear.

> "*We all fear pain and struggle, but they are often necessary for growth, and, more important, they don't present the level of danger that hopelessness and despair bring to us.*"
>
> **–BRENÉ BROWN**

Let's go back to the closet/basement analogy. Imagine everything of emotional importance in that closet had a name on it. Sorting out these undelivered emotional packages into personal piles and then sending them back to the appropriate person is a critical part of this journey.

To be clear—no, you do not need to *actually* contact these people. The real trick to this part of the UFB work is truly distinguishing who or what each package in your emotional basement authentically belongs to and accepting the fact that it is time to let them go.

Short-Term Gains, Long-Term Losses

Envision yourself in a library. You can go to the computer to find where a physical book is stored, but even if you were to delete or move the record of the book that is stored in the computer files, the real book would remain on the shelves and in the building.

Translating this metaphor to our experience—our body is the library, our brain is the computer. The book itself is both the internalized memories of our unfinished business and the *charge* those memories activate. They are a package deal; they're wired together. Charge will remain stored in the body even when we tell our brain we have come to terms with something from our past—even when we think we have pushed it out of our minds completely. We cannot just delete our unfinished business from our brain, because our bodies have the originals stored deep within them.

Dr. Levine states in his book *Healing Trauma: A Pioneering Program for Restoring the Wisdom of Your Body*: "Between the person and the memory of our feelings about a particular event (or series of events), we may deny that an event occurred, or we may act as though it was unimportant. For instance, when someone we love dies, or when we are injured or violated, we may act as though nothing has happened, because the emotions that come with truly acknowledging the situation are too painful. In addition, dissociation may be experienced as part of the body being disconnected or almost absent. Frequently, chronic pain represents a part of the body that has been dissociated."[16]

The goal here is to gain awareness of what our underlying feelings are in a given moment and what our habitual

responses to those feelings are. If we don't learn to identify these underlying feelings, we fall prey to a nasty habit:
ordering our lives around behaviors that may allow us to
produce an outcome we desire in the moment but do *not*
serve us in the long run.

Several years ago, I tore my rotator cuff and had recon-
structive surgery. As an advanced yogi, that was a very big
blow to my life. It was emotionally painful and hard for
me to accept such a loss of control over my body. I didn't
let it derail me completely—I continued to do yoga—but I
changed my practice to favor my injured shoulder, doing
whatever I could to minimize the pain. I was convinced I
had to *find a way to avoid the pain and to keep going*, so I
compensated by putting more weight on my good shoulder.

What was the problem with my approach? That constant overcompensation with my stronger shoulder would
have eventually changed the way my muscles developed. The
altered posture would have become permanently ingrained
in me—and that would have caused a chain reaction of
problems throughout my entire system. So, even though it
was helping me in the moment—allowing me to continue
the yoga practice I valued so highly—it would not have
served me in the long run. Fortunately, I realized what I
was doing to myself and stopped before it became a fixed
condition of imbalance.

This is what charge changers do to our experience of
our true selves. They help us avoid the momentary pain, but
when they become fixed states of being they stop us from
experiencing our full vibrancy and our true nature. Left
undiscovered and uncalibrated, they can create a permanent
misalignment in our souls and our lives.

We are going to examine how to identify your *triggers*,
the *charge* activated by them, and the *charge changers* you
reach for to avoid the discomfort caused by them—and

then to dissolve and discharge the associated energy and make different choices to take control of your reactions and outcomes. This is the act of moving from *charge changers* to *charge choices*—the choices we make from a clear and neutral baseline. This is the act of deeply and authentically getting to know the self. And it will have a dramatic, positive influence on your life. (Note: Triggers are not always obvious. In fact, they can be quite subtle. They can be background music, a sound, a smell, a place, even someone's hand or voice. Look everywhere.)

Overcharged vs. Undercharged

In order to learn to identify and release charge, we must grasp the fact that it comes in different forms. Let's look at charge and its types, "overcharged" and "undercharged," as well as how to identify what you do to suppress it in your efforts to create balance and control in your life.

When we are overcharged—like James, who froze at the sight of his brother hurt in the snow, or Chuck, who went in search of soft pretzels—we can feel anxiety, nervousness, fear, and the inability to focus, as well as the desperate need to calm ourselves. When we feel undercharged, we can experience lethargy, depression, lack of focus, and even a sense of immobility.

Being *overcharged* is when your body kicks into overdrive. Overcharge can show up as anxiety, anger, hyper-alertness, rage, overwhelm, shaking, dissociation, manic behaviors, ADHD, grandiosity, insomnia, a need for attention, difficulty breathing or thinking, or rapid heartbeat. It can show up in an instant with "hot thoughts" or an impulse to react, before you've even fully processed what's just happened.

Being *undercharged*, in contrast, is a drop in energy. Undercharge can be subtle or severe. Perhaps you feel tired, lethargic, lazy, or nauseated. You may feel zoned out, unable to make clear decisions, or disoriented; you may have a hard time getting motivated or focused. You may even feel paralyzed by overwhelm, or completely disinterested. Being undercharged can show up as a lack of animation, low body temperature, and feelings of being spaced out, withdrawn, quiet, tired, or numb. This can show up in different forms of depression, deflation, or avoidance.

Do any of these seem familiar? Take a moment to really consider that question.

Common Charge Changers

Below are a few of the most pervasive charge changers. Notice how subtle—almost invisible—they often are, seamlessly woven into our behaviors, reactions, and even our culture.

✵ SPIRITUAL AND INTELLECTUAL BYPASSING

Spiritual bypassing is a term introduced in the early 1980s by John Welwood, a Buddhist teacher and psychotherapist. I would define it as the false belief that with a sufficient relationship or deep connection to God, as well as any spiritual idea or practice, we can sidestep our pain, sorrow, and unfinished business. Similarly, *intellectual bypassing* is the false belief that with enough cognitive understanding of why something happened, or enough gathering of information around different psychological healing modalities and the functions of the ego, our healing will spontaneously occur. Whichever form of it you favor, you likely use bypassing in your own life; it is one of the most popular charge changers there is!

Once these beliefs and behaviors act as a sort of balm to smooth over our pain, we continue to use them more and more. An intellectual or spiritual bypass is like any other bypass—it is a detour, a way around the natural struggles of life in all its uncertainty and possible suffering. It favors the act of thinking over the act of being; it uses a feeling of connection with spirit or reason to avoid engaging with the pain and suffering of heartbreaking experiences.

It is fair to assume that we have all been raised in environments that have some level of aggression, hostility, disappointment, and heartbreak in them. We intuit early on that we get hurt and feel pain because we have bodies that experience both physical and emotional suffering. The skill of lifting our energetic and emotional field out of the body and into the brain is an early mastery of survival. Cerebral activity becomes the go-to choice over emotional pain. Remember when I killed my goldfish and I bypassed my feelings to be a part of my family's experience? They laughed and told me she was in a "better place" (relationship with God) and I could fix it by getting a new fish (reason and logic)—and I, not knowing what else to do, went along with it. For most of us, this becomes a habitual behavior early on: cognitively and spiritually anesthetizing yourself feels like a darn good option when your heart is broken, after all.

This kind of adjustment makes sense, right? Who wants to be in pain? Thinking is a way of numbing ourselves: ideas don't feel, thoughts don't hurt, plans don't weep! The numbing effect of the brain makes life easier—or so we think. However, in truth, this is a short-term strategy. Intellectualizing emotional experiences and internal bodily sensations tricks us into believing we have the ultimate control over painful situations—but what we really need to be doing is feeling and healing.

The biggest trap of this behavior is that it can come across as strong, impressive—in some cases, evolved or superior. Our culture lifts it up as a sign of intelligence, of success. However, when this behavior is a tool or a crutch and not pure enlightenment, it can ultimately cost us profoundly. By definition, a bypass is a secondary channel that allows a flow when the main channel is closed or blocked. Let's think about this definition, especially the notion that a bypass is used when "the main channel is closed or blocked."

One of our main channels is the vagus nerve. This nerve runs from our Root Brain all the way up to our Royal Brain (more accurately, the reptilian part of our brain—the brain stem—not the thinking brain) and has a great deal to do with our body's subtle communication system. The vagus nerve has fibers that innervate virtually all our internal organs, and it's what facilitates the management and processing of emotions between our three brains—the heart, brain, and gut. (This is why we have a strong gut reaction to intense mental and emotional states.) Bypassing is a route we take when the main channel is blocked—when we fail to recognize our bodies as the critical conduits for interpreting or processing information that they are and either intellectualize or ignore any painful information being relayed by the vagus nerve. This can create a total disconnect when it comes to our instincts, intuition, imagination, and emotional life. It also impairs our ability to be seen, appreciated, and chosen by others. If others cannot see our losses, our triumphs, our failures, our heart's longings, our ability to love, or our authentic selves, then they cannot see *us*, and therefore they cannot *choose* us.

Typically, after heartbreak, most people go into a spiritual or intellectual bypassing that reasons them away from their pain or disappointment. This charge changer bypasses the painful experience and acts like a life preserver that keeps our emotional heads above water. But that's as much as it can do: keep your head above water. It can't take you back to shore—back to safety and resolution.

When something resides in us for a long time, we think we've put it to bed, but the truth is that it's still there within us, finding ways to reorganize us. Until we've totally dealt with a past experience, it will remain alive in our bodies and nervous system, just waiting for us to pull on its thread and bring old, unresolved charge to the surface.

Here is the other kicker: this kind of unresolved charge is cumulative—and very detrimental. Pull one thread, and you pull them all. I referred to this earlier as the "emotional hairball" that keeps us choking but cannot seem to come up and out. You can't just wait for it to dissolve on its own; you have to tweeze it out and pull it apart, strand by strand.

✸ THE BLAME GAME

I love this quote from the late Gary Shandling, "I've been meditating for thirty-five years, so I can meditate until my mind is pretty empty, pretty blank, but then there's no one to blame." It makes me laugh every time I read it—and, more important, it connects what I am saying about spiritual bypassing to the concept of blame.

Ah, blame! It's one of our biggest charge changers. If you consistently let charge and your deep avoidance of pain and responsibility get in your way, you will continue to blame other people and circumstances for the things only you can repair. We can build cases against anything or anyone forever if we let ourselves—always without resolution or success. You blame, you're blocked.

Years ago, when my son was around eleven years old, he got in trouble for something he did at school. When I sat down to talk to him about it, he said that what had happened was everyone else's fault, not his. I had the nerve to ask him if he felt that he was at all to blame, and I will never forget his response: "Mom! Don't you understand when things like this happen everyone needs at least fifteen minutes of blame before they can take responsibility? Give me my fifteen minutes!"

Does that resonate with anyone? Do you remember the quote I shared earlier from Lewis Carroll's *Alice and Wonderland*—"That's right, Five, always put the blame on others"? Boy, do kids start young!

Our tendency to affix blame is deeply attached to our defenses against feeling *shame*, our most primitive pain point. Shame—this feeling that we are unworthy, inadequate, or, quite simply, *bad*—can destroy our self-esteem and make us want to run off somewhere to hide. In its most heightened form, it can make a person want to disappear. Shame is at the root of every addiction. Think of all the shame issues that people experience: body shame, beauty shame, money shame, shame around credentials and education, occupational shame, just to name a few. Since the advent of social media, we've even invented and deeply solidified a few more, like selfie shame and "likes and followers" shame. It's endless.

The story of Adam and Eve is a perfect shame-and-blame story. After they ate from the tree of knowledge, they knew they defied God, so what did they do? Yes, they hid! In response to their sudden awareness of their "nakedness," they hid from God. And what happened when the Lord asked them about it? Yup . . . Adam blamed Eve and Eve blamed the snake! Talk about original feelings. Even ancient wisdom understood the power of blame and shame and the threat of being unloved or abandoned by the people we desire to love us the most—the people we believe we need in order to survive.

When we focus on the *triggers* that activate shame and not just the act of who or what is being shamed, we shed a more useful light on this juggernaut emotion.

Questions to ask yourself:

- Do you default to shame thinking?
- What triggers it?
- When you experience shame, what does it feel like in your body?

It's an interesting exercise to check yourself on this one. The emotional and moral brain systems that are hard-wired into us judge quickly and unconsciously. Lashing out at others allows us to redirect our sense of shame and save us from the full experience of that pain. We case-build to protect ourselves; when we blame others, our sense of worthlessness and wrongness is projected outward rather than inward.

> *"It is clear that we are two different people—one of them conscious and the other unconscious."*
>
> **–JOHN E. SARNO**

Blaming can also be internalized toward the self, of course: people who tend to self-blame tend to assign anything negative that occurs in their lives to their perceived worthlessness or inadequacy.

Remember, as we touched on in Chapter 8, guilt is different than shame and is understood to be a separate emotion. Guilt—remorse at the suffering we may have caused another—involves empathy and regret and can inspire the act of apology and forgiveness. Shame does not. Shame and guilt can, however, be experienced together. You may feel shame for something you are guilty of, right? However, the primary concern in the emotion of guilt is on the suffering of the person who has been hurt—it focuses on who was hurt and the act of recovery and forgiveness—whereas shame runs for cover. As I mentioned before: Guilt is I *did* something wrong. Shame is I *am* something wrong.

People who are stuck in the experience of shame cast blame on anyone but themselves—whatever they can do to obscure their focus not on whatever "bad" act they've committed but on the "bad" person they believe themselves to be. Desperate for absolution, they cast about for someone to place responsibility on—at the expense of deep and honest self-reflection.

(A quick note about hurt and anger as charge changers: Hurt and anger travel everywhere together; they are quite the bedfellows. Think of anger as hurt's bodyguard and hurt as anger's salve or balm. Hurt smooths over anger and makes it more passive. Many people struggle with forgiveness because they believe anger is power, but it's quite the opposite: anger actually weakens the spirit. Both anger and hurt are big charge changers and huge deflectors when we feel the overwhelm of deep pain and shame. We must let go of anger if we want a truly empowered life. Anger, hurt, and blame are our smoke signals to dig deeper and deeper still. There can be some serious heartbreak and shame under there.)

Taking Total Responsibility: Revisited

This is a such an important concept for all of us to understand so that we can keep moving, growing, and healing in our life that I feel the need to revisit it. The idea that we are totally responsible for ourselves and our lives is sometimes a tough pill to swallow. You might be thinking to yourself, *My wife left me—how is that my responsibility?* or *My mom got cancer and died—how is that my fault?* I do understand what you are saying. However, if something is touching your life, it's part of your journey—and at the very least you must own the idea that your reaction to everything that happens to you is in your hands.

Our lives are about choices. Our lives are not the responsibility of our parents, past relationships, age, jobs, the economy, or the weather. We are responsible for every decision and choice we make. Do not be a victim to your circumstances, ever. That will dilute your potential and chances at pure happiness and well-being. When we don't accept personal responsibility for our circumstances, we greatly reduce our power to change them. Bottom line: We have two primary choices in our quest to deal with the unpredictable chaos of life: 1) we accept our conditions as they exist, or 2) we completely accept responsibility for changing them. You are the only person getting you to where you want to go; you are the only author of your story, and you are the only person qualified to write the ending to that story. Period. When you take full responsibility for your life, you will discover just how powerful you truly are. It is all in your hands.

Please take a moment to think about the meaning of total responsibility, as well as the areas of your life where you may have been avoiding it.

Lesson 3 Homework: Understanding and Diagnosing Charge

This homework is not complicated, but it is detailed. During the next five to seven days or so, you will need to keep a close eye on yourself, your behaviors, habits, and reactions. Ready? Let's go.

❂ STEP 1: IDENTIFY YOUR CHARGES

Let's start with a basic three-brain technique I like to use with my clients: I want you to take a moment each day to examine what you're feeling and what your three brains are telling you. When you feel reactive, uncomfortable, irritated, bored, scared, anxious, impatient, or charged— or, conversely, tired, disinterested, low-energy, lazy, or depressed—find a place to sit quietly. Pay attention to your body. Take deep breaths. Scan from Root Brain to REAL Brain to Royal Brain and see where your energy is active or may even feel trapped. Ask your Root and REAL Brains if they want to share anything with you and your Royal Brain. Ask them if they have any words regarding the situation at hand that they can share with you.

At any time during this week when something upsets you, notice where you feel energy, tension, movement, or other sensations in your body. Close your eyes. Plant your feet on the floor. Notice what's happening in your body. Notice where the energy is. Notice what words are coming up for you. Be aware of the shorthand the *body brains*—the Root and REAL Brains—use (words like *ow*, *help*, *sad*, *lonely*, *angry*, *hurt*, etc.). You may feel sparks or tingling sensations. And there may even be other words or sensations: *warm*, *moist*, *cold*, *empty*, and so on. Spend the next week or so practicing being aware of charge and how it manifests in your body and what triggers it. Remember, there is nothing wrong with the things you feel. This is your body naturally at work, letting you know it is alive and has its own needs and opinions. *Charge* is your body's way of saying, "I am here, and I need you to listen."

When charge arises, notice what you reach for, who you want to talk to or see, what food or drink you crave, or what you find yourself doing and thinking. What urges or lack of motivation do you experience?

You can also do this in reverse. When you notice your-self habitually or unconsciously reaching for something or moving toward an activity, ask yourself, *What is going on below the surface? What is my body trying to make me aware of? Can I put a voice to it?* You don't have to do anything else but notice the charge as it arises, stay with it, and then let it go. If something comes up, trust it and check it to see if all three brains are in alignment about it, like a compass pointing in a clear and accurate direction. Are you on to something? Are emotions coming up?

I remember the first time I started listening to my body brains. I wept and I had no real idea why at first—but as I continued to use this tool for discovery, my dialogue with the soma got clearer and clearer and I began to understand what was happening under the surface. Allow the charge to complete itself. Don't run from it.

It's uncomfortable at first, I know. Allow yourself some grace and spaciousness. After a session that brought up a lot of charge, one of my clients found that she was unable to drive home. Instead of panicking or trying to force herself to move, she let herself sit in her car for a while and experience everything she was feeling. Slowly, the charge worked its way up from her gut to her heart, then to her throat, and eventually out of her body altogether.

This is a lifelong practice that will take time to master; I don't expect you to notice every occurrence of charge in this first week. Don't rush it; be gentle. Just like pulling weeds in a garden, if you just yank at your charge, you won't get the whole root. Go slow, be thorough, and take your time. Trust yourself. Your body knows. Your body knows it all.

Every time you engage in this practice, when you come back into the present moment, take notes about what you've discovered.

"When suffering confounds us, we need to ask ourselves: whose feelings am I actually living?"
—MARK WOLYNN

✹ STEP 2: IDENTIFY YOUR CHARGE CHANGERS

Now that you've examined your charge and your modifying behaviors (charge changers), think back to the last time you felt emotional, angry, hurt, stressed, drained, overwhelmed, overcharged, or undercharged. What did you do to make yourself feel better? What did you do to change your charge? What did you do to relieve your discomfort? As we've discussed in this chapter, these are your charge changers.

This week you will also pay attention to your behavior. Any time you feel something negative, disturbing, or charged (over- or under-), and find yourself acting to suppress or distract yourself from that feeling, stop and ask:

- What am I feeling?
- What am I doing?
- Why am I doing this?
- What is causing this sensation or behavior right now?
- Why am I avoiding or abandoning myself and these sensations and feelings?
- Can I stay with it and let it complete itself?

Reflect on these thoughts and keep a journal. Then organize your discoveries on the chart provided (download and print at www.unfinishedbusiness/worksheets, or feel free to make your own).

Reminder: charge changers (dysfunctional charge patterns) are defined as distractions or actions taken in order to change or avoid the uncomfortable and often painful feelings caused by heartbreaking or traumatic experiences and unfinished business. We use these to shift the charge and avoid discomfort in the body—but in doing so, we stop the charge from completing itself. That energy becomes trapped and stored inside our bodies, hidden until a trigger comes along and makes us repeat our learned avoidance and coping behaviors.

Examples of charge changers:

- When I am stressed or depressed, I eat or drink or smoke_____.
- When I feel belittled, I start arguments with strangers.
- If I do poorly on a test, I distract myself by playing video games.
- If I feel scared or lost in life, I do yoga, read spiritual texts, drink a kale smoothie, or meditate in order to feel in control again.
- When I get lonely, I shop online or spend hours on TikTok.
- When I feel worthless, I spend money.

Some examples to help you along your way:

TRIGGER & CHARGE: When I get a text from my ex-boyfriend who dumped me, I get a sick feeling in my stomach. My hands shake and I begin to sweat—almost as if I'm about to vomit.

CHARGE-CHANGING BEHAVIORS: I get up and start to pace. I eat carbs—I can even down an entire bag of chips without thinking. Other times I get dressed up and go out and talk to guys to prove I'm still worthy and beautiful.

TRIGGER & CHARGE: I feel edgy and short-tempered, and I can't relax after work.

CHARGE-CHANGING BEHAVIORS: I drink four glasses of red wine and watch TV for hours, *or* I pick a fight with my wife and watch the game.

TRIGGER & CHARGE: I feel bored and lonely, which makes me feel nervous and scared.

CHARGE CHANGER: I lie in my bed and I start thinking about the job I left. Then I start to regret every decision I've ever made and tell myself my life is horrible and will never be good again. I self-punish and isolate.

On a personal note: After my mother died all I wanted to do was go out, talk on the phone with friends, or clean my house. I did not want to be alone with my pain and thoughts. The frozen charge in my body made me literally feel claustrophobic, like I was suffocating. I had learned all my life that being strong for others was more important than self-care and the deep reflection that leads to healing. Once I understood what was occurring and learned the process of releasing charge, however, my life changed for the better in dramatic ways. So please, dig deep and look closely. It's worth it.

CHARGE: What were you feeling?	MODIFYING BEHAVIOR to move/control the charge.

Tips for How to Process Charge

In the chapters ahead, you will be going deeper into the work, and as you do, you will experience charge. You may notice this through a feeling, or you may notice it via a charge changer—self-doubting, the urge to drink or eat, or even the impulse to throw this book at the wall or in the garbage. You may notice that you are in resistance and looking for reasons to not complete these exercises. Push on!

Remember, charge changers are the flag on top of the land mines. If you see the flag, you know there is charge. Instead of plowing ahead and letting the grenade blow, try to stop, sit, and process. Taking deep, even breaths along the way, ask yourself:

1. What am I feeling?
2. What am I telling myself about this feeling? What story is attached?
3. What am I afraid will happen if I stay with this feeling?
4. Am I telling myself the truth?
5. Can I sit with this and let the charge go? Can I let it complete?
6. Can I recall a time when I have felt this before? Can I follow this emotional artery back to a root experience—to its origin?

When you've asked yourself all these questions, take notes on any fresh or new awareness. Now examine your issues and then remind yourself, *Wait a second: I'm not being abandoned, I'm not inadequate, there is no danger here, the old story I tell myself may not be true.* Then ask yourself, *When did I start believing this? Can I breathe, release this energy with love, and move forward?* This is literally a way to start creating new neural pathways in the brain, and what science now knows is that "what fires together wires together." Said another way: when you start teaching the brain that when charge comes up and out, new messages can come through, and real and permanent change occurs!

Moving into Charge Choices

If we want our lives to change, we must make different choices. If we want to understand how we've created our present reality, all we need to do is examine the choices we've made in the past. Therefore, it stands to reason that as we become aware of our triggers, our charge, and our charge changers, we gain the power to change our charge changers into charge choices. If your charge changer is drinking tequila or throwing a tantrum, you can identify this as a pattern, check yourself each time you're tempted to engage in that behavior, and choose differently. *Our choices are the distributers of our energy and our power in this lifetime on this planet.* Maybe you want to read that again!

> *"Between stimulus and response there is a space.*
> *In that space is our power to choose our response.*
> *In our response lies our growth and our freedom."*
> **–VIKTOR FRANKL**

When you learn to examine the choices you make and *why* you're making them, as well as how choosing differently will create significantly different (read: better) outcomes, your life will become one of your own making. Diagnosing your choices is a tool for future self-empowerment and successful life design.

Bottom line: No matter what surfaces during the next few weeks (or months!) of this work, *keep going and keep writing*! Be aware of your charges and charge changers, and know that you have the absolute ability to choose and move into charge choices!

Homework Follow-Up

Questions to ask yourself:

- What are the choices I have made in my life that have led me to where I am today?
- Why have I made those choices? What "fueled" them? Were they mostly conscious and deliberate, or unconscious and impulse-driven?
- Can I get past old stories and patterns, stop reacting to my present with charge-changing behavior, and commit to making conscious charge choices daily?
- Am I ready to take responsibility for all the choices I make in my life from this point on?
- Are the choices I am making now moving me toward or away from a compelling future? Do they inspire me or deplete me?
- Are my choices in service of my short-term or long-term goals? Are they for me, or am I making them to please others?
- Is this choice in the service of my own and others' highest good?
- Am I making my choices from a place of neutrality?

Higher Self-Talk

I embrace the idea that I am an energetic being and that energy is the part of me that is always active. Sometimes this energy can feel blocked, and other times it can feel like it's too much. Over the course of my life, I've learned ways to cope and to try to control this life force. I developed behaviors so I wouldn't have to feel pain, disappointment, or discomfort. I now understand that these charge changers have helped me survive in difficult times, but at this point they no longer serve me and are keeping me from fully expressing myself—keeping me from the life I long to live. I am committed to honoring my body, my energy, my soul, and all that it communicates to and with me. I am no longer afraid of these feelings, and from now on I will allow myself to feel what needs to be felt, know what needs to be known, and change what needs to be changed. I can now allow every charge to complete itself through my body and be released for good. I am dedicated to fully examining and making choices from a place of self-understanding and deliberate intention. I am ready to take massive action around the conscious choices I make so I can create mindful outcomes in my life and free myself of old habits and distractions that don't support my highest good.

Chapter 10:
Lesson 4

*G*rowing up, both of my parents worked. Even though they had pretty good jobs, they couldn't afford help. Starting at around the age of six I was left alone each day to let myself in from school, lock the door behind me, get myself a snack, and then find a way to occupy myself. It was scary, and very lonely.

I watched a lot of television those first few years; then, when I was old enough, I got heavily into gaming. This lasted for my entire youth. Some of my best gaming friends were people whose faces I'd never seen (and still haven't to this day). I ate a lot of junk, drank a lot of soda, and became a chunky kid, which impacted my self-esteem.

As I got older, I struggled to connect with people and develop deep relationships. To be honest, the only place I really felt safe and confident was in my basement with a controller in my hands. As I isolated more and more, I could feel myself slipping into a truly lonely place.

I started doing the UFB work in my thirties, and what I found so fascinating was the awareness that most of us never really examine why we are the way we are and how we are shaped by so many things we never even think to question. As I developed the ability to really examine my *choices and why I make them, and to deeply understand that I wasn't born this way but was molded into these behaviors, a light bulb went off. I realized that my parents did the best they could with what they had. It was time to stop looking back and wishing things were different, time to release my anger toward them, and time to start healing and growing from today, from me, now. But most importantly, I had to own the fact that the past could never change and the only the power I had was to take responsibility for everything in my life and to make choices based on a whole new set of criteria.*

This changed my whole worldview. I was like a new person. It was kind of weird, actually. I'm not sure why we don't learn this stuff in school. I mean, almost everybody has been raised in a less-than-perfect environment, everybody is dealing with something, but we are almost blind to seeing where and how we got moved off track from being our unaltered selves. I use this work all the time. If I struggle with something or someone, I do a chart and let it go. It's like a secret weapon. I've shared it with many of my friends, and I hope to be able to help more people with it someday.

–DAVID

When most of us think of the impactful events of our lives, we typically think of the things at the epicenter of our unfinished business. We think of the obvious—the loud, earth-shattering, life-shaking events that have stopped us in our tracks and turned our world around. We don't think of the slow drip of wearing behavior, or the consistent relationship dynamics that erode our self-esteem, mute our intuitive voices, and shut down our inner compass. Nor do we think about which parts of ourselves we have specifically lost—we tend to look at our experiences as an amalgam of emotions rather than looking individually at the different tendrils involved. We rarely, if ever, ask ourselves investigative questions like, *What did I actually lose? Did I lose my sense of trust, my self-love or self-confidence, my dignity, my courage, my sense of love and intimacy, my faith in myself or others?* We also don't spend much time thinking about the things attached to our losses, such as coping behaviors, self-denial, and destructive habits.

But we're going to start doing all of this now—because gaining this awareness is critical to healing our hearts and our lives.

In this lesson, we will go deeper into unearthing these details. We will examine the experiences and relationships that formed us—the events and behaviors that structured our foundation and shaped us into who we are today. We will start to unveil why we see and interpret the world the way we do and why we react so intensely to certain life circumstances instead of meeting them with equanimity. We are going to scrutinize our programming and programmers—our patterns and our pattern makers, the people who planted our garden. We will also look closely at the two different types of stressful, impactful, or even traumatic events, and we will "out" the stressors and resentments that tip us off to the unfinished business causing them. We will get a full picture of the relationship dynamics and experiences that carved our hearts and built our walls.

We will finish this chapter with a completed map that will display the weaving of our inner world and help us clarify its impact in different areas of our lives. Be forewarned: in order to truly uncover all your heartbreaks and losses—*all* your unfinished business—you must be completely honest with yourself around your past and the relationships in it and unveil all your secrets, including those things you have always been afraid to think, feel, or say even to yourself.

This process is about coming clean, no matter how it makes us appear to ourselves or others. We typically categorize the negative things that happen in our lives by simply logging the stories, or the people who star in them; in the work we'll do for this lesson, however, we will get specific about the *types and categories* of losses we've suffered, and the ensuing resentments and indicators that have shown up in our lives—not just the people who are at the center of each story. And once we've finished assigning the traumas we've experienced to their proper categories, we will dig even deeper to review and pinpoint the mantras, behaviors, beliefs, charge changers, and AACTs that were created by and for each one.

This lesson is rich with data about why we are the way we are and about the *patterns* and *programming* that were created long ago. This is the chapter where we organize our past and the emotions it carries, just as we might organize a closet. The more specific we are about naming and organizing these types and categories of losses, the more we loosen their grip on us. Organizing and accurately positioning our inner life brings fresh awareness, clarity, and the opportunity to create space for the new, as well as the freedom to discard the old.

But first, let's understand the difference between *acute* and *chronic* trauma.

Acute vs. Chronic Trauma

When I was studying psychology, I became endlessly curious about the impact of chronic trauma versus acute trauma on children and their development. I suppose this topic was fascinating to me because I had suffered both in my own childhood. So many of the studies I read confirmed my belief that different types of loss, adversity, and stress could affect a person's life both in the present and long term.

It's no surprise that growing up in difficult circumstances can be hard on children and lead to behavioral issues and learning problems. However, researchers are now realizing that something even more damaging occurs for these children. Many studies have shown that ongoing stress during early childhood—poverty and neglect, addicted parents, difficult family dynamics, consistent chaos, emotional abandonment, and other adversity—can stay hidden beneath the surface, harming children's brains and other bodily systems. The research suggests that this can lead to some major disease in adulthood, like heart attacks and diabetes, as well as issues with anxiety, depression, and social dysfunction—proof that these constant drips of chronic damage stay with us for a lifetime if not fully addressed.

....

In his book *The Myth of Normal: Trauma, Illness, and Healing in a Toxic Culture*, Gabor Maté talks in depth about the two types of trauma I want to discuss here (though he uses different terms for them). The first is what Maté refers to as "capital-T trauma," or what I call acute trauma. He references two of my teachers, Dr. Peter Levine and Bessel van der Kolk, in his definition of the term, writing that it "involves automatic responses and mind-body adaptations to specific, identifiable hurtful and overwhelming events, whether in childhood or later." Ven der Kolk also defines trauma as the experience of not being "seen or known."

Painful things happen to nearly all of us in our lifetimes, but for the many who are made victims of neglect, poverty, oppression, racism, and outright abuse, the outcome can be severely detrimental. What I find so powerfully disturbing is that trauma (acute or chronic) is barely acknowledged by mainstream medicine and psychiatry, except for cases involving PTSD. Maté says this about "capital-T trauma":

"It underlies much of what gets labeled as mental illness. It also creates a predisposition to physical illness by driving inflammation, elevating physiological stress, and impairing the healthy functioning of genes, among many other mechanisms. To sum up, then, capital-T trauma occurs when things happen to vulnerable people that should not have happened, as, for example, a child being abused, or violence in the family, or a rancorous divorce, or the loss of a parent."

Events like these are at the foundation of the seminal study conducted on Adverse Childhood Experiences (ACEs) by researchers Vincent Felitti and Robert Anda between 1995 and 1997. In this study, researchers interviewed adults on the topic of childhood adversities and toxic stress, including abuse (physical, sexual, or emotional), family mental illness, substance abuse in the home, violence against the mother, incarceration of a family member, difficult divorces, and emotional and physical neglect. The researchers discovered that the more ACEs a person experienced in their childhood, the higher the likelihood of future negative physical and mental health outcomes—their effects are cumulative.

ACEs are far more common than we think. The CDC states that approximately 61 percent of adults experience at least one ACE before the age of eighteen, and that one in six report having experienced four or more. ACEs have the ability to over activate a child's stress response system, which is known to wear down the body and brain over time. "The damage that happens to kids from the infectious disease of toxic stress is as severe as the damage from meningitis or polio or pertussis,"[17] says Dr. Tina Hahn, a pediatrician in rural Caro, Michigan. Nadine Burke Harris, author of *The Deepest Well*, writes of how, when you put a child who has experienced ACEs in an MRI machine, you can see "measurable changes to the brain structures."[18]

Acute trauma, clearly, is serious and has far-reaching effects. But there is a second form of trauma that is far more universal—the kind Maté refers to as "small-t trauma." He states, "I have often witnessed what long-lasting marks seemingly ordinary events—what a seminal researcher poignantly called the 'less memorable but hurtful and far more prevalent misfortunes of childhood'—can leave on the psyches of children. These might include bullying by peers, the casual but repeated harsh comments of a well-meaning parent, or even just a lack of sufficient emotional connection with the nurturing adults." These events (or nonevents) are what I refer to as instances of *chronic* trauma.

It is obvious to most of us that bad things happening in our lives can have negative outcomes, but there is also the condition of "good things not happening to us," as Maté puts it. Things like emotional needs not being met or a child feeling unseen or unheard can not only lead to a disconnected, fractured self but can also rewire the brain to search for protection rather than connection. They damage our feelings of belonging and our relationship to the world. Trauma in all forms is, in its simplest essence, a fracturing of our being. These so-called nonevents are what the British pediatrician D. W. Winnicott referred to as "nothing happening when something might profitably have happened."

The more chronic forms of trauma happen over time and create subtle, internalized, and often imperceptible changes. They change our view of reality and, because our adaptation to these silent shifts happens so quietly, without our noticing, can redefine us and make us believe that the residue of our traumas is actually "just the way we are."

(An important side note: It does not always have to be just one or the other. Sometimes these two types of traumas can be indistinguishable from each other—they can seamlessly blend. Events can be both chronic *and* acute.)

Traumatized children may or may not show heightened signs of stress, and as with everybody, the constellation of symptoms these traumas set off can present differently in different people. But what is critical to understand is that children can be impacted powerfully by both types of circumstances. It's also important to note that different children are more or less sensitive to different categories of loss—one might suffer more from a loss of safety and trust, while another might experience a loss of dignity and self as a greater trauma.

I bring this up here because I do not want you to misunderstand loss, change, heartbreak, and unfinished business as only acute and sudden losses like a car crash, a person dying, a painful breakup, or a loss of a job or finances. Within this work, it is equally as critical to examine the long-term behaviors, relationships, and circumstances that erode our relationship to ourselves, our lives, and others as it is to examine the acute traumas we've experienced.

When my client Samantha was nine years old, the water heater in her house stopped working. Her mom didn't have the money to cover a repairman (let alone the emotional and mental bandwidth to deal with the situation). The whole family was taking cold showers and baths for months. Samantha knew that her mom was never going to do anything about it, so she finally called her grandfather and asked for a loan; found someone to perform the repairs and made the appointment; and missed school that day to let the person in and make sure the water heater was fixed. Can you imagine how scary and stressful it was for her to have to be responsible for her own safety, for letting the repairman in by herself, and for ensuring the repairs were done well? And this was not an isolated event: situations like this occurred regularly in Samantha's life.

In adulthood, Samantha suffered from both depression and anxiety and struggled to develop healthy long-term relationships. Her fear of being let down—as she had been throughout most of her life—kept her from forging true intimacy with others. She never felt safe counting on anyone else.

One might think that the impact of acute traumas like car accidents, a fire, the death of a loved one, the loss of a beloved pet, or a sudden, unwanted move from friends and community would have far more damaging results than what we think of as chronic stressors—food scarcity, verbal abuses, trickery, controlling behaviors, lack of support, and so on. But not all heartbreaks that impact our lives are clobbers to the head. Most often, our pain comes from a daily drip of the unbearable, of frustration—of "If I don't do this, no one else will" and "My survival, and that of those around me, is all on me."

Sometimes these traumas come into our lives long before we are capable of processing them—as they did for David, who at the age of six became a "latchkey" kid. Some come into our lives much later, as happened for one of my clients. His wife of thirty years told him every day what a loser he was—and after about five of those years, he believed it. His productivity collapsed, and he stopped reaching for his dreams.

Regardless of what's happened or when, all our experiences change the way we perceive, react to, and function in the world.

Acute heartbreaks and losses are generally easy to pinpoint because most (not all!) are one unforgettable event in time that typically plays over and over in our minds. For example, remember my surgery when the doctors used ether instead of full anesthesia? That's an example of an acute loss. (Note: because I was so young when this occurred, I hold it as a body memory, not an intellectual, detailed memory.) It was a sudden loss of control, of trust, and of safety. Similarly, when my client Miranda was dumped on her birthday by the love of her life—that was an acute loss.

Chronic heartbreaks, in contrast, are repetitive—sometimes occurring over years or decades, and sometimes to the point of seeming normal or expected. For example, when I was growing up, my sister played tricks on me every day. She also hid my belongings frequently and insulted me constantly. This behavior, though it may seem like kid stuff, deeply impacted me because it was a *chronic* loss of love, trust, safety, and dignity—it happened over and over again.

We can also feel the loss of things in our life that we *didn't* want. Sometimes we leave a job or end a relationship knowing that it's the right thing to do, but once we leave for good we feel confused, uncertain, scared, sad, or even full of self-doubt. We might miss the positive aspects of that job or relationship. We may romanticize what we left behind, amplifying the good and minimizing the bad. This kind of loss often feels like regret or even resentment, but it's not. It's the grief that comes from unfinished business, and the disorientation that goes along with it. These experiences are loss experiences, just like getting dumped or being tormented by a sibling.

Trauma is not an easy thing to spend our days thinking about. Most of us would rather master techniques to avoid doing just that. However, for the sake of this work—for the sake of our own healing—this is what we must do daily until our job is complete and we are whole, healthy, and happy again. To do this work well, we must go deep into the center of ourselves.

I want to make clear that unfinished business is not always as easy to find as it seems. We think of these things in a way that puts them in a "gross" perspective—the big-ticket items we see in the movies or read about in books or hear in the songs we listen to. Yes, those things are certainly worthy of inclusion—but heartbreak is often more subtle and more complicated than that. The smaller and more consistent losses in our lives can act like noise machines, lulling us to sleep and blocking out life's natural sounds altogether with their synthetic drones.

We can also experience profound growth and positive change after loss and trauma. We grow and heal from heartbreak when we investigate it and understand it at a much deeper level—it can give us a sense of meaning and purpose. The work of Richard Tedeschi, PhD, and Lawrence Calhoun, PhD, on post-traumatic growth (PTG) established that people who endure psychological struggle following adversity can often see growth and change. These people experience a kind of transformation following trauma. "It's not just bouncing back," says Tedeschi. "Most people talk about that as resilience. We distinguish [it] from resilience because this is transformative."

We need to go below the stories and the noise we carry in our minds and move down to the level of the actual loss issue our body is experiencing so we can find it, name it, and release it. This work helps us to zero in on the heart of our life. Then we can let the real song and voice of our soul come through. This is when clarity and healing can begin.

Putting Words to Feelings

The act of truly getting to know ourselves, the light as well as the dark, is life-altering. Having the ability to go deep, without avoidance or bypass, into our shadows and our most deeply buried parts, is key to living and loving fully.

Part of this diving-down is learning how to name our pain. There is a line in Shakespeare's *Macbeth* that is so simple and yet truly profound: "Give sorrow words." Shakespeare was on to something—studies show that explicitly naming our emotions reduces our psychological response to them; it literally reduces activity in the amygdala and lowers the skin conductance response. You know those sweaty, creepy feelings you get in your skin and belly when you're scared or stressed? By labeling what the emotional stimuli causing those feelings are, we take the sting out and the fear/stress itself dissipates.

Emotional labeling, also called *affect labeling*, provides emotional clarity and gives us a deeper understanding of our experiences. Naming our emotions and being specific about the stimuli and details surrounding them is an absolute game changer when it comes to moving into healing, because it bridges the gap between thoughts and feelings.

Dr. Michelle Craske and her coauthor, Dr. Matthew Lieberman, both UCLA professors of psychology and of psychiatry and biobehavioral sciences, are the authors of the first study to demonstrate the benefits of affect labeling. They had this to say upon the study's publication: "The implication is to encourage patients, as they do their exposure to whatever they are fearful of, to label the emotional responses they are experiencing and label the characteristics of the stimuli—to verbalize their feelings. That lets people experience the very things they are afraid of and say, 'I feel scared and I'm here.' They're not trying to push it away and say it's not so bad (aka intellectual bypassing). Be in the moment and allow yourself to experience whatever you're experiencing."[19]

They went on to study how this approach could help people who have been traumatized or have suffered highly impactful life events. "I'm far more optimistic than I was before this study," Lieberman said of their ongoing research. "I'm a believer that this approach can have real benefits for people. There is a region in the brain, the right ventrolateral prefrontal cortex, that seems to be involved in labeling our feelings and our emotional reactions, and it is also associated with regulating our emotional responses. Why those two go together is still a bit of a mystery. This brain region that is involved in simply stating how we are feeling seems to mute our emotional responses, at least under certain circumstances." Craske adds, "That is so different from how we normally think about exposure therapy, where you try to get the person to think differently, to think it's not so bad. What we did here was to simply encourage individuals to state the negative."[20]

With these findings in mind, it's clear that categorizing our unfinished business is critical. If we simply state, "I was betrayed and my heart got broken," we miss the opportunity to be specific about the event that occurred and the things that made us feel—and we need that specificity if we want those feelings to loosen their grip on us.

Let's look at an example of how this works: If your father told you every time you got a B-plus on a report card that you were a failure and would amount to nothing, you might feel great anger toward your father and carry the story that the two of you couldn't get along or nothing you did was ever good enough. You may also carry the story that no matter what kind of effort you put in, you will always be a failure and remain unseen by your father and others.

That is the broad-stroke story of your relationship, but let's zero in on the details so you can understand that more things are happening underneath the surface. Let's look at each tendril of this experience and get you a specific understanding so you can move toward absolute clarity and forgiveness, and finally release the energetic memory in its entirety.

That experience with your father can be broken down into six loss categories. In that relationship dynamic you were:

1. Losing faith in your abilities.
2. Losing self-esteem.

3. Losing trust in your "tribal leader."
4. Losing trust in your own personal compass.
5. Losing faith in the belief that you could build a life in the world as an adult.
6. Building a relationship with shame and losing personal dignity.

Notice there are at least six different loss issues in this one relationship!

In this lesson, you are taking the first step in regaining your power around your past.

Remember, *we leave our spirit in the unhealed places of yesterday.* This lesson's work is meant to *organize* your impactful life events, large and small, so you can clearly see what is still alive in you today, what remains unresolved from the distant and recent past, and what is acute or chronic. We'll also be looking at which specific categories these events fall into and which specific parts of ourselves have been lost, broken, or impacted by each one. This process also includes reviewing and notating when our AACTs, MMBs, and CCs began, and why.

The Four Rs

This lesson's purpose is to review our lives and stories while being mindful of the four "Rs": ruminating, reminiscing, retrenching, and reflecting. We are going to reflect on our lives from way up—taking the thirty-thousand-foot view—so we can bring order to our significant life events without getting stuck in one place, story, or mythical hurt.

When we *ruminate*, we become deeply reflective in thought and can become stuck and unable to move forward. Our thoughts tend to become all-consuming and never find a resolution. We find ourselves focusing on negative, low-vibration experiences, which prevents us from seeing events neutrally. The practice of rumination can be fueled by anger, grief, anxiety, or negative feelings and emotions.

When we *reminisce*, we tend to remember and contemplate our past from a charged and romanticized place. These memories come from an emotional state that does not give an accurate perspective of an event. The level of emotions involved distorts the facts and we look at everything through rose-colored glasses rather than a clear, balanced lens.

Retrenching is the act of reliving our past over and over, which feeds into its negative energy. We adopt heavy and deliberate case-building, and often very inaccurate storytelling. Reliving the details repeatedly in this way digs the grooves of these memories in deeper and deeper. This is not good for letting go or achieving forward movement.

Reflecting, on the other hand, is the act of thinking about an event or events from the past, reviewing the story of your life without judgment or embellishment in an effort to understand, organize, and find clarity. When reflecting, you're moving toward neutrality; this is your truth, and this is where you want to be. This is a lighter, crisper, more accurate approach to reviewing the past than any of the other Rs can ever hope to be.

> *"It isn't a matter of forgetting. What one has to learn is how to remember and yet be free of the past."*
> **–ALDOUS HUXLEY**

Studies show that ruminating on past events versus reflecting takes you out of a healing space, making it challenging to unpack your past and reorganize your major events into categories. Ruminating brings us to the shadow side, where we keep telling ourselves, "I'm not good enough, and that's why this and that happened . . ." *Reflecting* on the facts, on the other hand, allows us to halt our false narrative, rewrite it, and redirect ourselves. It puts us back into the seat of awareness and choice—no more fairy tales, mythical hurts, or stories of self-pity. This is what we want: the facts without the fluff.

Lesson 4 Homework: Completing the Puzzle of You

We will start from the beginning: your childhood. Taking what you now understand about acute and chronic loss, labeling emotions (our loss categories), and the coping characteristics (AACTs, MMBs, and CCs) we've developed from our UFB events, let's work on creating what I like to think of as a completed puzzle of the self.

✸ STEP 1: INVENTORY ORGANIZATION

Review your homework from Lesson 1, when you wrote for four consecutive days about all your impactful events, heartbreaks, losses, and unfinished business. Remember when I said that it was important that you were honest and factual, and didn't let it become a long, drawn-out story? If you skipped this section before, I suggest you go back and complete it. If you did it before but feel like you want to take another stab at it with fresh eyes, do so now.

When writing, it's important to go back to date the significant losses, changes, or transitional events you're recording. Try your best to put them in chronological order. Do *not* include any emotion, romanticizing, or elaboration. Just create them as bullet points, in as accurate of a timeline as you can manage—but if you are not certain about specific dates or times, don't worry about it. (It can be helpful to have a notebook handy, or another document open on your computer, to take notes of any new awareness that comes up through this process.)

After you're done reviewing the first draft of your Lesson 1 homework, highlight or circle any events that still feel painful or active right now.

It's important to list everything that comes to mind—and remember, they don't all have to be explicitly negative events. Transitions, changes, dramatic moves, graduations, the birth of children, marriages, going to college, empty nest, and so on can all be forms of loss. For example, the greatest gift of my life was having my son, Gideon, but embracing that gift also meant that I experienced a loss: I left my career as a successful actress to raise him, ending a familiar and celebrated part of my life. Let's also not forget about the loss of things in our lives that we *didn't* want in our life, like the toxic people, things, and experiences that were hard to let go of despite the fact that they were detrimental to us or hard on us.

Don't leave anything out. If it hurt, left a mark, or changed the trajectory of your life, or even if you simply still find yourself thinking about it or telling stories around it, then it's worth noting!

The list you're creating should be a diagram of your life from the perspective of *heartfelt organization*. Think of it like you're flying over your life—snapping photos of all the challenging or impactful events that affected you, taking notes on them, organizing them, and zooming in on the areas where you want to know more details.

In this section we want to stack and organize your losses, changes, and transitions so they are clear and easy to dissect. Examine if they were only heart-*breaking*, or if they were also heart-*helping*. (Remember: we do not want to *ruminate*; we only want to revisit!) Using the chart on the following page, make a comprehensive list—*without* ruminating, reminiscing, or retrenching!—of these events. Label each one as either chronic or acute, and note at what age they took place. We'll be working with this list throughout the rest of this chapter.

✺ STEP 2: THE FIVE MOST IMPACTFUL LOSSES

Now that you have listed all your losses, heartbreaks, and transitions—both chronic and acute—I'd like you to select five that seem to be the most impactful so that we can categorize and further analyze these losses. Remember to review the work from Lesson 1 to jog your memory. When you've made your choices, record them in your journal.

✺ STEP 3: CATEGORIZE

Now I want you to think of these losses in terms of categories—remembering that each one can belong to several different categories. If we're going to heal from a loss, we need to get it out from the root—the whole, entire root. Every loss has several tendrils, and until we unearth, confront, and deal with each one of these categories, we'll continue to carry around the pain and the charge.

Note: I have narrowed down the categories in the chart provided to twelve; I affectionately call them the dirty dozen. If these twelve do not fit your circumstance, however, keep in mind that there are many more in the appendix at the end of this book.

Pick *one* loss, heartbreak, event, or transition, and then categorize and organize the various associated losses in the chart provided here (download and print at www.unfinishedbusiness/worksheets, or sketch out your own version on a piece of paper). Repeat this for each one of your "top" five losses, heartbreaks, or transitions.

Again, remember they don't all have to be negative! Anything that has had an impact could be one of your five!

A great example for you to consider here is a client of mine who became a mother at a young age. While giving birth to a healthy, beautiful child is a life-affirming event and she has a beautiful daughter now, when she became a young, single mother, she lost her freedom, her career (she was forced to drop out of grad school), her people (her family didn't approve), her romantic relationship (the baby's father left), her dreams, and her identity (recently a free-wheeling student, she was now a mother). She also lost her financial security and safety, not to mention her faith in God, her sense of trust, and her dignity. Her one transition resulted in at least eight different categories of loss.

Chronic loss has different categories as well. During the COVID-19 pandemic, we all experienced a chronic, ongoing loss, as well as a number of other losses both chronic and acute—of jobs, of financial security, of trust, of health, of control of our bodies, of a sense of safety and/or belonging, and of community, not to mention a sense of normalcy and routine. Some also experienced the tragic loss of a loved one or loved ones.

Again, take one loss, change, heartbreak, or transition (acute or chronic) at a time and categorize all the different losses within it, utilizing the chart provided, and repeat the process for each of your five losses.

Examples:

ACUTE: My sister was killed in a tragic car accident. I never saw or spoke to her again. This acute loss created in me: 1) Loss of trust and safety; 2) Loss of faith; 3) Loss of a loved one; 4) Loss of belonging, as she was my closest sibling; 5) Loss of dreams that included all the future life events I hoped to share with her.

CHRONIC: My client Dave spent his childhood alone and lonely as a latchkey kid. He had a daily drip of fear, boredom, loneliness, and responsibility far beyond his years and skill set. This created in him: 1) Loss of safety; 2) Loss of self-esteem; 3) Loss of power; 4) Loss of identity; 5) Loss of belonging; 6) Loss of relationships; 7) Loss of dignity.

What traumas or transitions in life have you not thought about in this way before?

Let's begin to take an inventory of your losses, heartbreaks, deep disappointments, and transitions (to help broaden your categories and organize your losses, please review the list located in Appendix 1 as well as the sample chart in Appendix 3). On the next page you'll find the dirty dozen:

LOSS CATEGORY

1. Loss of power (energetic or real)	2. Loss of trust (betrayal)
3. Loss of identity (including sexual)	4. Loss of self (esteem)
5. Loss of dreams/time (abstract)	6. Loss of faith in G-D / Humanity/ others
7. Loss of control (body, mind, circumstances) (abuse)	8. Loss of Finances or financial security (energetic or real)
9. Loss of safety (emotional or physical)	10. Loss of a loved one or ongoing relationship/ patterns/familiarity (wanted or unwanted)
11. Loss of belonging/tribal acceptance (tribe of origin or of choice)	12. Loss of dignity and the onset of shame

"I am not what has happened to me. I am what I choose to become."

—CARL JUNG

✦ STEP 4: PUTTING IT ALL TOGETHER

Now that we are clear about our top unfinished business events—which ones are acute or chronic, and what categories they fall into—we will finish our chart off by naming which coping skills, charge changers, personality traits, beliefs, behaviors, and AACTs came out of each event. There was a specific time when we started reaching for coping mechanisms. Some came early (sucking our thumbs, watching TV, playing alone, being smart), some later (drinking, sex, masturbation, anger, exercise), but we all do *something* to self-soothe or distract when we're feeling triggered. When did our coping mechanisms, charge changers, or creative adjustments start? When did we create our AACTs? When did we start believing what we believe, and who taught us to believe it? Who modeled those behaviors and beliefs for us?

In this exercise we're going to use these questions to break down your unfinished business so we can get a clearer understanding of what your triggers are, when they were created, and who was involved. This part of the work will bring you many "aha" moments about behaviors you may have never been able to put your finger on before. It will allow you to connect the *when,* the *where,* the *how,* the *who,* and the *why* to the *what.* It will bring more clarity as we move forward (and at this point in the work, we all know how important clarity is, right?). It will also help you to establish a diagnostic process you can use on all of your patterns as you move forward in your life.

Every loss, heartbreak, and transition has associated MMBs, AACTs, CCs, and relationship(s) attached, as well as what I call stress indicators—physical symptoms that tell us we're stressed and in need of attention (e.g., your skin breaks out, your hair falls out, your stomach hurts, you get sick a lot, you get migraines or UTIs, you drop things, forget things—please review the list I've provided in Appendix 2 for more examples). Again, we're just adding another level to our understanding of our losses and UFB and how they show up in our bodies and behavior so we can see in full detail the many layers of their impact on us.

A chronic loss suffered by so many lately were the lockdowns necessitated by COVID-19. Putting together everything we've learned here thus far, let's examine this loss and the many layers related to it that we may have experienced during the pandemic in this sample chart:

LOSS #1: COVID LOCKDOWN

ACUTE OR CHRONIC	BOTH ACUTE AND CHRONIC
MMBS	**MODELS:** Isolate and don't talk to anyone. (Modeled by Mom all my life.) **MANTRAS:** "I have no right to complain. Other people have it far worse." "You're so weak. Everyone is handling it." "This is what happens when you make plans." "Nothing works out for me." "Just my luck" **BEHAVIORS:** Stay indoors and don't let anyone see my sadness. Be supportive of all my friends without asking for similar support, because I'm "the strong one."
AACTs	"I've got this all under control. I am the best at quarantining. My Insta followers love all my self-deprecating jokes and posts."
CHARGE CHANGERS	I drink every night because I feel so alone and anxious. I stay in bed until noon. I watch the news all day.
STRESS INDICATORS	I can't sleep at night. I've gained ten pounds and my hair is falling out. I keep forgetting things. I bite my nails.
CATEGORIES OF LOSS	All the different losses I have experienced as a result of this one loss are:
LOSS OF POWER	When will this end? I have no idea. I can't control any of this!
LOSS OF TRUST	Weren't our leaders supposed to protect us? We are not safe!
LOSS OF IDENTITY	Who am I if I am not at work or out with my friends?
LOSS OF SELF	I don't even know who I am anymore or what I like to do. All I do is watch television. I've lost all ambition.
LOSS OF DREAMS	Goodbye vacations, my wedding, my girls' nights out, concerts with friends . . .

LOSS #1: COVID LOCKDOWN

ACUTE OR CHRONIC	BOTH ACUTE AND CHRONIC
LOSS OF FAITH	Where is God in all this? Why are so many people sick and dying?
LOSS OF CONTROL	I have no idea what to expect or count on anymore. No one does! Will I catch it? Will I die?
LOSS OF FINANCES	My income has been dramatically reduced / I lost my job.
LOSS OF SAFETY	I am scared to grocery shop, see friends, or even leave my house for fear of getting sick or getting someone else sick. The world is falling apart!
LOSS OF A LOVED ONE	I've lost my friends, neighbors, coworkers, experiences. My aunt/grandfather/cousin/friend died.
LOSS OF BELONGING	Who am I without my people? Is Zoom all I have? I need a hug!
LOSS OF DIGNITY	I should be doing something with my time and life. What's wrong with me that I am taking this so hard? I feel so ashamed of myself. I'm a hard worker; I can't believe I'm on unemployment. How did I become such a loser?

See what we've done here? We've taken one loss—a mass of tiny, interconnected roots—and separated out every tendril it contains. It's like putting our loss under an MRI machine for a 3D picture; whereas an X-ray could give us only a two-dimensional, monochromatic view, an MRI can see everything: where the blood is flowing, where it's blocked, where repairs are happening, what parts of us are compensating to stabilize it, and what it looks like in all dimensions. In essence, it fully weighs the situation in its entirety.

To fully understand the depth of our losses, we need to look at them in their totality and understand how they have shaped us. Remember, this is a constellation, not a fixed, one-dimensional experience.

You'll repeat this process for all your "top" events. Reminder: Follow the charge—the red flag on top of the land mine. If a feeling comes up, sit with it. Follow the tips in Lesson 3 for dealing with charge so you can continue to move through and stay with this very important work.

So now it's your turn. You're going to fill out the following chart for all five major losses/transitions you picked in Step 2 of this exercise. If you feel the top twelve loss categories do not fit your loss, please look at the full list of losses in Appendix 1or create your own headings. Trust your instincts and intuition. Listen to *all three* of your brains!

This homework is a culmination of everything we've done together in Lessons 1–4. This is your chance to take a fully multidimensional view of your major events and losses.

Again, you'll need to complete this chart five times—one for every event/trauma you've selected to examine here. You can download and print this chart at www.unfinished-business/worksheets—or, of course, you can simply sketch it out for yourself on some blank pieces of paper.

Have your five charts ready? Okay, here we go:

ACUTE OR CHRONIC	
MMBS	MANTRAS: MODELS: BEHAVIORS:
AACTs	
CHARGE CHANGERS	
STRESS INDICATORS	
LOSS OF POWER	
LOSS OF TRUST	
LOSS OF IDENTITY	
LOSS OF SELF	
LOSS OF DREAMS	
LOSS OF FAITH	
LOSS OF CONTROL	
LOSS OF FINANCES	
LOSS OF SAFETY	
LOSS OF A LOVED ONE	
LOSS OF BELONGING	
LOSS OF DIGNITY	
OTHER	

Homework Follow-Up

This was a lot of work. Congratulate yourself on diving deep and doing the necessary (but often uncomfortable) work of digging up the roots of your emotional weeds—I'm sure it wasn't easy. Things you've never consciously thought about before have likely begun to surface for you, and you may find that after the work you did for this lesson, certain aspects of your life will no longer be tolerable. You may find that things you have been quietly tolerating for quite some time—relationships, careers, behaviors—no longer feel right. You may feel out of sorts.

Yay! Congratulations! It's working! You're moving charge. You're waking up to what you genuinely want and who you truly are, and you're ready to begin letting go of all the stories, losses, heartbreaks, traumas, old beliefs, models, mantras, and AACTs that you've been holding onto and hiding behind for far too long.

Questions to ask yourself to help you get clear on the many aspects of the grief you likely feel bubbling up right now:

- What pain am I still holding onto that I wasn't aware of before?
- Who comes up for me in these memories? What people were responsible?
- Do I hold resentments toward any of the people who have caused me this pain?

It's not only okay to acknowledge your hurt, it's important to do so—and remember, it's important to notice the *who* that comes up when considering all your losses too.

Higher Self-Talk

I am grateful for the insights this lesson's work has brought me. I have experienced and tolerated many traumas throughout my life—acute and chronic—and still I have endured. All along the way, I've done the best I can with the wisdom available to me. The MMBs, AACTs, and CCs I adopted so I could survive and make my pain more bearable have served me well, and I offer gratitude for their support throughout my life. However, it's time to let them go and to move on. I now understand my patterns, and with the help of my body's wisdom, I can clearly see my triggers and my reactions to my world and the people in it. There is a lot I have been hanging onto, and I'm now willing to complete it all. I am ready to release the pain, the charge, the charge changers, and the behaviors that no longer serve me. I am ready for the next phase of my life journey. I am devoted to the process of releasing the unfinished business of my past. I am committed to creating the future of my soul's desire.

Part III

Chapter 11:
Recap

In the previous lessons, we've taken a deep dive into the societal and familial expectations and relationships that bind. We've evaluated our original story, identified the UFB we've been carrying around, and explored why it "matters" to us and to our future. We're now aware of the models, mantras, beliefs, and behaviors that have come from our families, communities, and authority figures. We've also discovered our AACTs and our deep need to belong, as well as our charge changers. Then we put it all together in Lesson 4, giving ourselves a complete, holistic view of our unfinished business and the many ways it shows up in our day-to-day lives—our minds, bodies, and souls.

In the next few lessons, we'll be moving through to the center of our being to the sacred core of our relationship to unconditional love, emotional and internal power, and compassion. Next, we'll move into our *heart*, which will allow us to transform our energy into something higher so that we're free of what keeps us stuck and what keeps us blocked. We'll learn to reflect on and then release the old so we can move forward with absolute clarity and meaning. Free of the old, worn-out stories of hurt and heartbreak, we'll move into what I call the "safe stories" that support a neutral past and an enlightened future.

Let's return to our original question—the one that started this whole thing: Who would you be if nothing or nobody had ever gotten in your way or broken your heart? Who would you be if you were just the light essence, energy, intuition, connection, and love you were born to be? Who would you be if no one had influenced you with their models, mantras, and beliefs—if you'd never learned or developed any AACTs or charge changers? Who would you be if you just had a straight line of energy from your entrance into the world all the way through to your divine connection and purpose? Who would you have been without all that interference?

This is the work of these next few lessons. Through the last few lessons, you have become aware of all the interference; now you're going to start clearing it out—finishing your unfinished business.

As you do this work, you will begin to feel lighter— physically and energetically. You'll ascend from the root of your existence to the dizzying heights of your highest potential as a free and weightless soul. It's powerful stuff, and I'm excited to do it with you.

Let's go!

Chapter 12:
Lesson 5

My dad was a charming, funny guy. When I was a kid, I couldn't wait for him to get home in the evenings after his business dinners so we could spend time together. He would let me ride on his back like he was a horse. It was pure joy. When I got older, we would engage in colorful, animated discussions on an array of topics—history, finance, politics, sports, and even the latest hot TV show or music artist. He was smart and he was my best friend.

My dad was also successful. He'd inherited a manufacturing company from my grandpa, who'd inherited it from his dad. We had a great life in an affluent area of LA. We wanted for nothing. My parents were both highly active and respected in our community and in their social circles.

As I got older, I started to realize that the only time my dad was available to me was after dinners or cocktail parties, events at which he'd have quite a few drinks. As the years passed, our time together stopped being fun—well, he stopped being fun. He was quiet and sullen most of the time. Didn't want to be bothered. I started to notice he wasn't spending as much time with my mother, their friends, or me and my siblings.

Things really came to a head the day I found out I got into the college of my dreams. My father sat us down and explained that we didn't have the money—couldn't pay for a private college. I was devastated; my mother, meanwhile, went ballistic.

"Where is the money?" she demanded. "Where did it go? Where?!"

It got worse when my mother started hearing talk about my father gambling and spending time in public with other women and even prostitutes. We eventually learned that my father had spent, gambled, drunk, and "dated" our generations of family money away. My mother left him, and my world—our world—fell apart. My mother fell apart. I hated my father for years. We all did. Even with the "understanding" that he had a disease, I still felt rage and shame constantly. People whispered about us, and I struggled with anxiety and depression as they took turns inside me daily.

When I started this work, so many things became clear. I realized that we all have parts of us that are good and parts that are challenged. We all have weaknesses and strengths. We are all light and dark. What impacted me most was the wisdom I gained around honesty and forgiveness. Once I was totally honest about and forgave my father, it gave me permission to start again from me. Not him. I stopped mythologizing him and started taking full responsibility for myself and my life. I stopped blaming my father for, well, anything.

So much of what I believed about my dad was false—a projected, fantasized idea of my dad that I was not old enough to get clear about. Once I saw my father as human, fallible, and vulnerable, I began to love him again. I began to free myself from the past. I was able to live from an honest and authentic place. I had to say goodbye to the father I thought I had in order to build a relationship with the father I actually have.

My family still struggles at times, but I keep my heart and head clear by consistently doing this work. The charts help me keep my emotions in order so I can stay conscious about what is mine to clear and what is theirs to deal with on their journey. I feel blessed every day that I truly know who I am, and what I want. I own the fact that it's all in my hands now.

—JAKE

....

"One of the pitfalls of childhood is that one doesn't have to understand something to feel it. By the time the mind is able to comprehend what happened, the wounds of the heart are already too deep."

—CARLOS RUIZ ZAFÓN

Who Is Taking Up the Most Room?

When I was an actor learning technique to break down scripts and characters, I learned that it was critical to gain a full awareness of how the person had developed into who they were—what issues they struggled with, and what their life was like from early childhood until the present moment. Who was their family of origin? Where were they raised and in what conditions? What habits did they have? What car did they drive? Was their body injured? If so, where? Were they healthy? What were their significant relationships? What had they been through and where did they spend their time? Getting a bird's-eye view of a life is a brilliant psychological tool to gain an objective understanding of that life.

As a visual learner, I found timelines and charts helpful as I did this character breakdown work. In my later studies, I noticed that many modalities also use timeline work to give people clarity around a myriad of issues. They are truly great organizational tools. When I studied neurolinguistic programming (NLP) in particular, I realized the huge benefit of timelines, charts, and objective overviews. I now frequently use variations of those (mine are a bit more creative and fun!) in my work, with incredible results.

In this lesson, we'll use another chart to aid us in naming our individual relationships and identifying the unfinished business associated with each one.

There are so many events, large and small, that impact us in our lives, but typically at the center of each event is a personal relationship. This lesson will ask you to draw a clear picture of the first relationship that comes to *heart* as being the biggest and earliest disrupter of your energy and belief systems, as well as your unencumbered potential. Who is hurting your heart even now? Who is blocking your energy today? Who left you with the most all-encompassing stories and limiting beliefs? Who co-created your most enduring patterns?

We will create a detailed diagram of this person and look at both sides of your story—considering their strengths and weaknesses, the balance of good and bad in your relationship, the extent to which you have mythologized them, and more.

Let's take a look at the truth . . . all of it. No more stories without clarity—only facts!

One of the great blessings about creating a chronological heart chart is that we not only get to be super clear about how our lives evolved to where they are now but also start to get a real bird's-eye view of the ways in which our patterns emerged and were reinforced. The overview perspective of our powerful relationships also gives us a truthful perspective about who the important people in our lives are and were, and what was genuinely great and what was profoundly hurtful about our relationships with one another.

For years after my mother's death, my father talked about her as if she were a saint who had never done anything wrong. "Your mother never complained," he would say, or "Your mother kept a perfect house and she never asked for anything more than we could afford." A big one was, "We were crazy about each other." He never spoke about the fights they'd sometimes had, or the fact that she'd most likely wanted more out of life than she'd gotten. He also never mentioned her smoking or drinking. And he certainly never admitted that she was part of the generation of women who never spoke up for themselves.

Eventually, when I realized this perfect image he was preserving wasn't serving him, I (gently) challenged my father's rosy portrayal of their story. Although it was hard, my father gradually found a new and beautiful truth around his vision and memory of my mother and about their enduring but imperfect love for each other. This fresh perspective helped him heal from the loss because it was both honest and whole.

We must not fantasize or romanticize the people in our lives, or the stories that we lived out with them. No matter who you are writing about, if you find you only have happy memories or angry, sad memories, you are not telling the whole truth—and if you are not telling the whole truth, the body knows and will not release the charge it causes. It's like only taking out part of a splinter; what is left will fester, becoming worse over time. The body, mind, and soul want the truth, the whole truth, and nothing but the truth. Being completely honest is critical; incomplete truth leads to incomplete healing.

Years ago, I had a client who had been severely abused by a parent as a child. When we reviewed the relationship, they only wrote about negative events—totally understandable, given their history. However, when we dug deeper, many new realizations came to the surface. They remembered how that parent helped their education by being devoted to homework and discipline. They remembered ski trips and vacations, laughter and the love of chess. They remembered, in short, that there was some good intermingled with the terrible.

No one is all good or bad. The body knows that—and it needs the whole truth in order to release the whole story.

Gone but Not Forgotten

I never met my grandparents. My maternal grandmother passed when my mother was five years of age, and my paternal grandmother passed when my dad was in his thirties. Both grandfathers passed when my parents were teenagers. You would think I wouldn't even think about them, but whenever I would hear my friends speak of loving relationships with their Nonny or Grammy or Pops or Poppy, my heart would feel sad. I wondered what that must have been like, what having another generation of love and wisdom to wrap around my life would feel like. This is a simple example of a *phantom relationship*—an archetypal presence, so to speak, that never filled the space psychically and emotionally created for it and has therefore left a gap in our soul.

Most of us do not realize that important figures from our past remain an energetic presence in our daily experiences, and in our psychology and physiology, regardless of whether they are presently a part of our life. They can be found in the decisions we make or avoid, the people we choose or reject, the way we socialize or isolate, and all the phantom conversations we have in our minds. We all have relationships with people who are not present—particularly primary caregivers who have not remained in our lives, whether because of death or any other reason. Where that someone used to be, or was supposed to be, a hole remains; it is like having an invisible friend that just keeps breaking your heart over and over.

My client Dana grew up without her father, who left her and her mother when she was three. Dana does not remember much of anything about her dad, but she does remember the feelings of abandonment, as well as the depressed and fearful behavior her mother exhibited after being left with no money to raise her all on her own. This had a huge impact on Dana's life—though she never realized it until we did our work together.

Here is a metaphor that nature has given us: Have you ever passed a forest or grouping of trees and noticed, in the crowd, one tree that is growing at an angle, leaning and straining to reach for the light? That tree is being shaped by everything it *doesn't* have as much as it is by all the things it *does* have.

This work is designed to clear the forest so your soul can stop straining to survive and start growing straight up into the light of its potential!

Complete or Repeat

Now that we have sorted out our life events, we need to name the people and relationships those events were experienced with. We carry around our relationships, and the impact of them, like an internal GPS that determines the direction we follow every day. Have you ever responded to someone in a positive or negative way because they were "just like" your father? Mother? Sibling? Ex? The most important and complicated aspect of this part of your work is getting super clear around which events, situations, and patterns define the impact of these relationships, good and bad.

In our investigation, we start to remember things we may not have thought about through the lens of heartbreak, loss, change, or transition. *Creating heart charts is the act of taking one relationship at a time and examining them so you can fully understand them.* We will look at the most meaningful and significant people in your history to see where your patterns and programming developed, and we will pull apart events and experiences to understand their impact on you, your decisions, and your life, including in the present moment. We will examine your awareness around what you do and how you behave when you interact with the people closest to you as well as the strangers/acquaintances you come across daily. This is a truly intimate look at the people who have shaped us and how they show up in our lives and our behaviors to date. That includes the good, the bad, the beautiful, and the ugly.

Comprehension is not the name of the game here; *completion* is. This is the reason why talk therapy alone may not work in the healing of the past. When we do not fully complete our unresolved heartbreaks, our unfinished business, and our issues from childhood and beyond—when we do not release the energy our bodies still hold—we are doomed to repeat the patterns created by our past over and over again. Our unconscious will not have it any other way.

Lesson 5 Homework: Taking Responsibility and Letting Go

The purpose of this exercise is to discover long-held patterns of behavior and beliefs that were impactful and how each relationship contributed to, created, or co-created those patterns and beliefs. As always, it's important to be super clear and *profoundly honest.* None of this work will force you to address this person face-to-face; this work is about addressing your relationship with them, getting it clear, and releasing it *for yourself.*

"Our stories are not meant for everyone. Hearing them is a privilege, and we should always ask ourselves this before we share: 'Who has earned the right to hear my story?'"

—BRENÉ BROWN

✺ STEP 1: THE HEART CHARTS

Heart charts help us to identify the patterns of behavior and beliefs that routinely present themselves in our lives. They help us to gain clarity and objectivity around our development and the people who contributed to it.

To begin this process, select the relationship that brings you the most intense memories, impactful thoughts, and highest *charge*. This is often, but does not have to be, one or both parents, a close family member, or any primary caregiver from your life.

Remember, *none of this work will be shared with the other person*. This is for you and for your healing. The goal is to address your relationships, understand them and the charge held within them, and release that from your *"self"* and your *body*. Be authentic and go deep!

A few rules:

- Events should be bulleted and in chronological order. Try to put a date or age on each event. (Note: I said *try*. This is not a test, so if you can't remember, do the best you can and move on!)
- Do not leave anything of importance out. If one of your greatest memories of your dad is cleaning the garage, put it in. If one of the most painful memories about your mom was the fight you had when she wouldn't let you wear lipstick, put it in. Remember, this exercise is not just about super-huge, traumatic events.

- Go as deep as you need to and include what you intuitively feel is necessary to create a clear picture. Including five to ten events in each column is usually plenty, but if you find more, go for it.
- Include both positive (Bright Side) and negative (Shadow Side) experiences. If you only have good or if you only have bad, try again. Every relationship has both a bright side and a shadow side.
- Feel free to take notes separately on what feelings come up, but keep the chart clear and clean. If you discover a pattern, notate it. (Example: If your sister made fun of you all the time but you put down one event that was super impactful, please make mention of the fact that this was chronic behavior. Or perhaps your mom was your best friend, but she also made you dress in a way that made you self-conscious. Include it all.)

Many people struggle in this part of the UFB process with feeling guilty or resistant (*If I say that about my mom or dad, won't I sound ungrateful? If I give this person credit for the good stuff, does that mean the bad stuff doesn't count?*) Remember, everything here is for your own well-being. The person you are writing about is not there. You don't have to say any of this to their face. Leaving things out won't help anyone else; it will only hurt you. So put it all in, and do not bypass any of this—spiritually or intellectually. If you find yourself telling a story, stop. If you find yourself giving excuses or reasons why a person did what they did, stop. There will be time for that later. No amount of guilt will remedy the past, and no amount of anxiety is going to help you create a beautiful future.

This exercise is for *you* and *you alone* to release what needs to be released so you can let go and move on. Our success is only as complete as our honesty!

Here's a chart to help you get started (download and print at www.unfinishedbusiness/worksheets, or sketch out your own version on a piece of paper):

BRIGHT SIDE +	SHADOW SIDE -

❈ STEP 2: THE FOUR PATHS TO LETTING GO

My divorce was a challenging experience. Even when a marriage is not working, the loss of a dream, a family unit, a home, and a structure for your child is heartbreaking and, quite frankly, scary.

About a month after being on my own in the world again, I went to my first dinner party. I felt so uncomfortable. I had not been out as a single woman for over a decade; my party legs were shaky, and my whole body felt tense, frenetic.

After I left the gathering that evening, I pulled into my driveway, got out of my car, and sat on my front stoop. The night had been exhausting, but the evening air felt kind and comforting. I checked in with my body to see what it was trying to tell me. As I did, an inner voice, clean and clear, said, "Not all of this belongs to you, you know. Some of this is yours, some of this is his, and some is society's. Get clear. The world around you will know when this has passed."

Suddenly energized, I immediately went inside and created the lists you are about to work on for the second part of your homework.

A few days later, I went to see a therapist to talk about the changes happening in my life; I wanted to make sure I was handling it all as well as possible for my son. After we chatted for a while, he asked me, "How do you feel so healthy and complete around all of this?"

I laughed out loud at this, because I knew I was on to something. His words confirmed for me that the approach around healing the pains and breaks in life that I'd been cultivating for years was starting to culminate into something worth sharing.

I see it this way: No matter what has happened to us in our lives, every situation can be looked at from four different sides. Four perspectives. Four paths. There is the *personal*, the *impersonal*, the *mythical*, and the *global*. I like to call them the four paths to letting go. We all know every story has more than one side, right? And somewhere in the middle resides the truth.

Let's look at it like a box with four sides that carries the truth to wherever we want it to go and to whomever we want it to reach.

The first side (personal, *you*) we need to look at in every situation is the part we are responsible for. What do we need to acknowledge, take ownership of, and perhaps even humbly apologize for? Remember, taking responsibility gives us back our power to make things whole and healthy again—it gives us the awareness that, no matter what happens, we can at least make our part of it better.

The second side (impersonal, *them*) is letting the other person or people off the hook for the part they've played. This is simple physics: if we've got a hook in someone, they've got a hook in us! So let it/them go with grace and awareness. This is based in the mindfulness practices of acceptance and forgiveness—"I release you fully from _____." Give yourself the gift of forgiveness.

> *"Forgiving people doesn't necessarily mean you want to meet them for lunch. It means you try to undo the Velcro hook. Lewis Smedes said it best: 'To forgive is to set a prisoner free and discover that the prisoner is you.'"*
>
> **–ANNE LAMOTT**

The third side (mythical, *idealized or dramatized thoughts of the past*) is naming what you're carrying with you—e.g., "I have carried these thoughts and feelings in my heart and in my mind long enough . . ."; "I hate you. I love you. F**k you. I wish you would have / could have _____"; or simply, "I have always wanted you to know _____."

The fourth (global, *worldview*) and final side requires us to ask ourselves, *How will the world know I have let go and moved on from this, what will doing that look like, and what will I no longer accept as the status quo? What can the world no longer expect from me? How will the outside observer know that my life has changed—that I am creating and living by my own rules now? What will that look like from an objective viewpoint?* (We cannot dismiss the fact that the world around us has many long-standing social constructs, beliefs, and expectations that contribute to the way we feel about ourselves and others in any given situation or circumstance!)

Fill out this next chart with *one* person in mind. Remember—be open and honest! Write from your heart. Imagine the person is standing in front of you (while also reminding yourself that they aren't, which means you don't have to feel like you must hold back or "be nice"). There is no omniscient power judging you for feeling the way you do. There is no danger in letting yourself become aware of exactly how you feel! The purpose of this exercise is to unburden yourself of all the feelings you've held in and onto for so long. Again, as I mentioned above, *no* storytelling or intellectual/spiritual bypassing allowed. If you even *sense* avoidance or candy-coating creeping in, stop and check yourself. Now is not the time to make excuses for anyone—not yourself, not the person you're writing about. It's the time to be clear, honest, and courageous.

I am not asking you to write a novel or even a letter here (that will come next). The statements you write in this exercise should be direct and to the point—clear and cathartic. Don't be afraid to swear! Don't be afraid to say, "F**k you!" It's okay. Let it *all* out—now is your chance.

This self-expression isn't about getting back at anyone or about making some nasty point. This is about clarity around what was and what is. What happened and what's done. This is about the truth—the whole truth. This is about getting to every single one of the tangled roots you're trying to dig up. So much of our pain is connected to these attachments and stories we've been holding onto for most of our lives; now is the time to disconnect ourselves from them, once and for all. Let's turn that soil over. Let's plant a fresh, beautiful, weed-free garden.

As an example, let's return to my client Cathy, the divorced woman with several children, and her answers to the questions we're posing here.

What do you take responsibility for?

- "I take full responsibility for not speaking up and asking for my needs to be met in my marriage."
- "I take full responsibility for not asking for the truth about what was going on inside your head and heart."
- "I take full responsibility for not seeing the great distance between us or noticing that even our friendship was deteriorating."

What do you release them from?

- "I fully release you from the expectations I had of open and clear communication. I forgive you for hiding your truth and telling me everything was great."
- "I release you from my need to have the ending of our relationship be different. *We* are different people, with different ways of being in the world, and I now accept that."
- "I forgive you for leaving me with the tremendous responsibility of our seven children."

What do you want them to know?

- "I am very grateful for the lessons I've learned from this, and for the time I now have to experience true love and build the life I've always wanted. I am profoundly grateful for our seven children. I also want to thank you for the early years and the fun we had."
- "What you did hurt me. Oh, and by the way, f**k you for not giving me a heads-up and turning my world upside down like that. If you had been totally honest with me, you might have discovered I felt the same things, and we might have been able to handle it all differently. That would have served our children and families well."
- "Good luck in all you do. I only wish the best for you."

How will the world see a shift?

- "I love more deeply and experience life from a place of gratitude and excitement."
- "I walk confidently into rooms and ask for what I want, I share what I feel, and I am not ashamed of living on my own terms."
- "I am a leader. I understand and model that a woman can stand fully on her own and doesn't need a man on her arm to feel good or valuable. I am in total control of my destiny."

Note: When you fill out the "I want you to know" box, know that the sentences can start very differently than "I want you to know." The purpose of this box is to say the things you never got to say to them but wish you could have—the good and the bad (since no relationship has only good or only bad!). You can use "Thank you," "I wish," or "F**k you" to begin your statements, or whatever other structure that will allow you to say what you need to say.

You don't need anyone else's permission or approval to release these feelings or thoughts. The person you're writing to here may not even remember the things you've been holding onto, and that's fine—what matters is what's going on inside of *you*! You won't be saying any of this to the person's face, and that's a good thing; the last thing you want to do is give them the power to re-trigger old, dead issues. The unfinished business you're exploring here is yours and only yours to let go of now.

Let's get started (download and print this chart at www. unfinishedbusiness/worksheets, or sketch out your own version on a piece of paper):

I take full
responsibility for:

I fully release
you from:

I want you
to know:

How the world
will see a shift:

Homework Follow-Up

You have done something courageous. You've taken responsibility for your pain and your past. You're not carrying it all on your shoulders anymore. You realize there are many parts to a person and a relationship—that there are not just two sides to every story, there are many, and we're all multidimensional beings with multidimensional issues.

Learning to let go is never easy to do, but it's necessary in order move on. Take the time you need to adjust to this new lightness of being, of presence. Sometimes when we carry something for a long time, we experience phantom pain even after the pain has been brought into the light or removed. It can take a while for our body to adjust to this new way of being, and residual information and energy may continue to present itself throughout the next few weeks or even months. Be patient, and feel your way through this period. Soon you'll notice you have more energy to focus on what you truly want, rather than on things you don't want or others expect you to want.

Questions to ask yourself as you complete this lesson:

- Are there any energetic or emotional injuries in connection to the people you've charted about this week that you can still sense?
- What other relationships do you need to let go of and forgive? (Please list them.)
- Can you commit right now to forgiving them all and continuing this work to release them?
- What fears do you hold about letting people off the hook and taking responsibility for yourself? (Please list them.)
- Can you think of stories or beliefs that are preventing you from forgiving these people?

- Are there people that you have wounded that you feel ready to forgive yourself for?
- What are the loving and healthy relationships you have created and nurtured that are in your life today? (Please list them.)
- Is there anything that came up during this process that surprised you?
- Are any of the people you charted about this week still in your life? Do you feel ready to set boundaries with those people moving forward to develop a fresh and healed relationship with them and others?

Higher Self-Talk

I am ready to release and let go. I know what's mine; I know what's no longer mine—or perhaps never was mine. I know what belongs to the world and its expectations, and I will never follow that path again. I am free to move on, fully and wholly. I will no longer let the past have its hooks in me. I will no longer put my hooks into others or support situations that hinder my growth or my freedom. I am willing, ready, and able to put down the heavy load of my past and move toward becoming the person I am meant to be, was born to be, without any more interference from the outside world. No matter who or what that involves, I will create from a place of completion, neutrality, and full personal responsibility and integrity. I am fully integrated and ready to move on with a whole, healed, and healthy heart and soul.

Chapter 13:
Lesson 6

W*henever I would hear the song "If You Could Read My Mind" by Gordon Lightfoot, I would get upset. I had no idea why. None. One night I was in the car with my wife, and out of nowhere, she started singing it. I asked her to stop, and then I asked her to never sing that song again. When she asked me why, all I could say was, "I don't have a clue, or a memory. I just know that it makes me feel uncomfortable and makes me want to cry."*

Months later, after that incident in the car, one of my best childhood friends died. It hit me hard—not debilitating hard, but hard. I was sad all the time. My wife noticed. After a few months, she gave me the gift of the UFB work. I thought it was overkill, as I didn't feel that bad—just, well, sad. But I did it anyway, and she did it with me.

Man, what I discovered about my life, my past, my family, my beliefs, and the way my family communicated and grieved was enlightening and life-changing. There were so many things buried down deep. So deep I had no memory of them at all.

Here's the crazy part: as I was investigating my life, I found the Gordon Lightfoot issue! When I was a young teenager, my mother and father split up for a period. It was terrifying and heartbreaking. My mother was my world, and she was the one who moved out. I was so lonely, and my father was in no shape to be there for me. It was the year "If You Could Read My Mind" was a hit. My father played that song alone in his room and I could hear it through the walls. That was the hardest year of my life. I coped by burying it and becoming the perfect student and class president. I had no recollection of it until I did this work and dissected my life and my story. My mom eventually came back, and she and my dad worked it out.

When I wrote my letters and shared them with my wife, it was like a huge weight was lifted—one I'd never known I was carrying until then. She was so loving and compassionate; it brought us even closer. It is so powerful to think about all the things we bury down deep in order to survive. This work changed my life, my marriage, and all my relationships.

–NOAH

....

"If we want to be happier, we first need to allow unhappiness in. We have to be real."

–TAL BEN-SHAHAR

Deeply understanding our relationships and getting clear on their *authentic* stories is one of the healthiest things we can do for ourselves and the people we love. What's even more amazing is that releasing and sharing these understandings with a full, loving, and open heart may be the most profoundly healing medicine we can experience. In fact, science has shown that getting clarity around your stories and expressing that clarity from a place of vulnerability and complete honesty literally turns off the body's stress responses and short-circuits stress hormones like cortisol and epinephrine. It also turns on your body's relaxation responses and releases healing hormones like oxytocin, dopamine, nitric oxide, and endorphins.

A new brain-imaging study by UCLA psychologists reveals why verbalizing our feelings makes our painful emotions less intense. Matthew D. Lieberman, UCLA associate professor of psychology and a founder of social cognitive neuroscience, states, "When you put feelings into words, you're activating this prefrontal region and seeing a reduced response in the amygdala. . . . In the same way you hit the brake when you're driving when you see a yellow light, when you put feelings into words, you seem to be hitting the brakes on your emotional responses." In short, putting our feelings into words can actually help us heal better.

This sharing creates a condition of self-repair in your body, and it functions as a form of frontline therapy and preventative medicine. Engaging in this process creates a form of circulation and freedom for the body and its energy system to heal; it reminds your heart and soul that you are fully heard, worthy of your truth, and not alone. It relaxes the nervous system, helping to quiet and heal the mind. It has been shown to reduce symptoms of depression, anxiety, anger, and fear. It also helps you develop a deeper sense of belonging and connection.

Even more profoundly, when we get clarity around and say goodbye to the past, we make space for new possibilities to come in. What came before is over. Forever. Let the past be reborn into a fresh tomorrow. You will not forget, stop loving, or lose the memories. You will simply see them from the place of non-charged neutrality and gain the ability to redesign your life and purpose from a space that is not marred by the old and irrelevant.

Recharge to Discharge

It's time to resolve those old wounds and conflicts by saying goodbye to your old reality—a reality that doesn't exist anymore—to truly forgive what has happened in the past, and set it free. It's time to say, "I release you. I still love the blessings, and I'll carry the memories and honor everything you taught me. But it's time for me to pick up my heart and soul so I can move on. I am needed elsewhere." This way of saying goodbye frees you (and anyone else involved) from old stories that are serving no one; it is the best thing you can do for everyone involved.

In this process, we will say goodbye by writing a letter to each person that we've created a heart chart for in the last lesson. This exercise is highly effective for releasing charge from the energy system and body. If done consciously and carefully, it can get you beyond the stumbling blocks and emotions you never thought you could recover from. One of my teachers, Tal Ben-Shahar—a lecturer in psychology at Harvard and the author of the book *Happier: Learn the Secrets to Daily Joy and Lasting Fulfillment*—gives this wonderful note when it comes to writing: "The key is not just to write it down, but to write it down mindfully—to focus, to imagine, to re-experience!"[21]

Yes! To reexperience!

The purpose of *transactional writing* is to express and complete an exchange of feelings, thoughts, and long-held beliefs with someone else. It is a deep act of closure. We re-create—or, as Ben-Shahar says, "re-experience"—the feelings, and then we read this letter out loud in order to transfer energy directly out of the body; we *re*charge to *dis*charge.

When it comes time to read your letter, first make certain you are in a healing space where there isn't any pressure to act on anything or make intellectual choices around moving forward. Then focus on making the person in question as real as you can in the present moment. Find a photo to look at as you read; before you begin, take the time to deeply evoke their presence, just like an actor would call in the character they are playing. Let their imagined presence stir up real feelings. If you are working with a trusted friend, imagine them as your person as fully and authentically as possible.

Afterward, take time to let your body discharge. The charge you have around each person or relationship should release on its own—it's not an intellectual process—and it can continue to move for days, weeks, or even months following your completion. When reading the letter out loud (alone or to another person, if you have chosen to work with a trusted friend), emotions and possibly tears will come up. *Do not stop them!* Move through them. Shutting these deep emotions down—cutting off our free-flowing charge and the hurt that ignited it—is how we got ourselves into trouble to begin with. Let the emotions complete fully as they arise. Let the charge complete.

If you are with another person during this part of the process, do not reach out for them or let them reach out for you. When we experience physical touch, the central nervous system reacts, which can stop the charge from fully releasing. *Learn to let it go!* Cry it out if that's what shows up for you. Let your experience be full and unaltered.

After you're done reading, please take the opportunity to stay quiet. You will likely feel wiped out and tired. *Perfect!* Rest and release.

The greatest benefit of this work is felt when you show up with the complete truth, so please resist holding anything back or sugarcoating your story. Drop the AACTs and the masks and let the charge rise up and out! Let it go!

Saying Goodbye

"Holding onto anger is like drinking poison and expecting the other person to die."
–NELSON MANDELA

Why do we need to say goodbye? Because the relationship of old doesn't exist anymore. The past is exactly that—*the past.* Even if the person is still in your life, the old stories, hurts, and dynamics that were a part of your experience before don't need to be anymore. You can start energetically fresh!

As we've discussed, old hurts have very disruptive ghosts. Mythological hurts—old stories that grow and get bigger with time—become almost heroic and create a form of case-building against another person. These stories contribute to us being *right*, and they serve to place our relationships in a state of *woundology*—a place where you over-identify with and get stuck in your wounds and their energy. Most of us have a tendency to hold on to old hurts and traumas and even to define ourselves by them, ignoring our strengths and potential in the process. Woundology can keep you stuck forever—and serves absolutely no purpose.

We can't keep stirring up old, stale, dry dirt if we want a clean, beautiful, nourished garden—a fresh future filled with possibilities and love. We have to say, "I release you; I still love the blessings and hold on to the lessons. I'll carry the memories and honor everything you taught me. It's time for me to pick up my heart and soul so I can move on. My loving heart and I are needed elsewhere."

My clients will often get stuck on the idea of letting certain issues with someone go; they feel if they let them off the hook and release them from their envisioned outcome, they will lose all power over the situation.

As we've already discussed—*nothing could be further from the truth*. The truth is that if you don't embrace this "letting go," you will not heal. We have to forgive what has happened in the past in order to feel whole and happy.

People often confuse anger and hate with power; they believe that if they give up the anger and hate, they will lose their power over the circumstance. The truth of the matter, though, is that getting rid of anger and hate gives you *more* power, not less. The second you let all that go, you will feel empowered and energized.

Hate and anger exhaust your soul and diminish your impact in life. If you let them live inside you for too long, they will leave your spirit shattered and scattered. This work is about setting down our baggage, not sifting through it. It's about gathering up all the pieces of your soul that you have left scattered throughout your life and calling them back home. Remember, only total clarity, forgiveness, and responsibility equals real freedom!

> *"Your trials did not come to punish you, but to awaken you."*
>
> **–PARAMAHANSA YOGANANDA**

Lesson 6 Homework: Release Through Writing

Writing can be therapeutic for all of us, but it is especially therapeutic if you use a pen or pencil rather than technology. "Writing helps us track our spinning thoughts and feelings, which can lead to key insights," says Elizabeth Sullivan, a licensed marriage and family therapist with a private practice based in Australia. She describes the act of writing as "speaking to another consciousness . . . another part of the self. We come to know who we really are in the present moment." Writing is also profoundly effective in creating a connection between mind, body, and spirit, she says, and adds, "When you use your hands to pen or type something directly from your brain, you are creating a powerful connection between your inner experience and your body's movement out in the world."[22] I agree with this and would prefer you use a pen and paper at first to really deepen your connection to your three brains. If that's not your thing, however, and feeling like you have to do it that way is going to hamper you from getting this part done, no worries—type away.

✸ STEP 1: WRITE A LETTER

Using your heart chart and your four paths to letting go, write a letter addressed to your chosen person. This letter should be written from a deeply compassionate perspective, where you are taking full responsibility for what is yours, releasing them fully from what is theirs, and sharing what you never got to but always wanted to say. Then comes the last and best part: envisioning what the world will look like when you are free and clear of old, unresolved, residual emotions.

Be authentic in this letter. Go deep and tell the truth. Remember, once again, that *you don't need to show it to anyone.* The goal is to release both you and the other person from your old story and finish your business with them so you can live in a space of freedom and light. You can say "I love you" or "F**k you"—just tell the truth, whatever that may be! And make certain you do this from a place of true forgiveness and release. Remember, your body keeps the score; it knows if you're telling the whole truth and nothing but the truth, or fudging things. Leave nothing unfelt or unsaid.

Start by addressing them by name and offering your overall perspective on the relationship. Then introduce your reason for writing the letter. As you continue to write, make sure you include everything from your four paths chart.

Example:

Dear Mom,

I know you have been gone for years now but I don't think I have ever truly said goodbye to you or the complicated relationship we had . . .

There are so many things I want to share with you. There are many things I want to take responsibility for . . . [list them]

I release you from . . . [list them]

There are some things I always wanted to share with you, but we never had the time or I never had the courage to say them . . . [list them]

Finally, I know the world will see a difference in me now that I am free from the weight of our past . . . [list them]

No matter how long this letter goes, it should end with something along the lines of:

I release you fully, I still love all the blessings, I'll carry the memories and honor everything you taught me. It's time for me to pick up my heart and soul so I can move on. I am needed elsewhere. Goodbye.

Your letter does not need to look exactly like the example I've just shared here, but it does need to include all the information you have parsed out in our previous lessons and placed in your paths box. It can have more than what is in the box, but not less. You must also make sure you actually say *goodbye*.

You can be creative here. Some of my clients have written the most beautiful, poetic letters; others have just kept it clean, simple, and to the point. I even had one client who had lost his mother when he was a young child write his letter in crayon. Listen to your heart (and brains) and connect deeply with this process. You will be profoundly moved by this if you fully commit to and put your whole heart into it.

Note: These letters are not reserved for people only; you can write them to *experiences* too. For example, when I sold my business that I loved so much, I did a heart chart, four paths grid, and letter to process the loss and say goodbye. I was amazed by how fully it cleared me of any dwelling on the past or romanticized reminiscing. You can do this with jobs, dreams, homes, cities, and more. I recently did this work with a client who had to close his business due to COVID-19, and he said the weight it lifted from his shoulders was life-changing for him.

Let's begin writing our Dear UFB letter! Get a piece of paper or open a doc on your computer and let your words flow.

Note: Please complete this process for anyone or anything that you put on your lists—but keep in mind that, at this stage, you only need to start at the heart chart from Lesson 5 and move through the letter-writing process for each one—you do not need to restart at Lesson 1!

✸ STEP 2: REVISIT YOUR LETTER

When you're finished writing the letter, the process isn't complete. Leave the letter for a few days and see if any new awareness comes to you—things you didn't think of before that you may want to add. When you are ready (or even if you feel resistance but know there's more to say), come back to it. Find a photo of the person you wrote your letter to or call a friend you trust fully or call your therapist or coach to share it with and read your letter aloud. As best you can, imagine that you're in the room with the person you have written to. Feel their energy, embody their spirit (this is almost like an acting exercise), and then read your letter aloud like you're reading to them. If you do not have a photo but do have an object that reminds you of that person, use that. If you have neither, just conjure up a clear picture of them in your mind and heart.

You should feel charge while writing or reading the letter, but if you feel flat or disconnected, please take the time to revisit your heart chart and the paths to letting go so you can consider what may be missing or things you didn't address completely. Talk to your three brains. Get their input. There may be a big issue you are avoiding and don't want to unearth, and your body knows it. This is the time to dig in and get it out.

Go deep, mean it, and share your truth!

Homework Follow-Up

You have done amazing, life-changing, soul-healing, ener-gy-shifting work. Be patient. Feel what you need to feel for as long as you need to feel it. Remember, this is not an intellectual process, so there's nothing more for you to do right now than wait for the charge to release on its own! All this work is moving energy up and out of the body, and the reading of these letter is literally a transfer of energy directly out of the body.

It's entirely possible that you'll feel this energy con-tinue to move for days or weeks or even months following this step—but the freeing of internal space should happen on its own, so if time passes and you still feel incomplete, please reread and retrace. If writing or reading the letter has effected no change at all, you most likely need to redo your charts or letter and go even deeper. Don't beat yourself up, though! There is no right or wrong way to heal or let go. This is a process. And sometimes the process requires us to do things over—to go even deeper.

Keep in mind that you may have a delayed reaction to this part of the process. Some people don't feel energy moving while reading the letter aloud, only to find themselves crying or shaking or in a very sour mood hours later. That is energy moving itself out! Honor the process. Honor yourself. You're doing deep work. You're letting go so you can move on and grow.

Some things to ask yourself and to reflect upon after you've completed and read your letter:

- What does the act of committing to speaking your truth, now and in the future, mean to you?
- Check in with your three brains and see if you have left anyone off your lists. Get clear on the reasons for possible resistance. Then add them.
- How often do you express yourself honestly?
- Do you have trust or belief in something greater than yourself that can help you heal and grow and share your heart?
- How much do you trust your own counsel or any outside guidance if it does not guarantee the outcome that you want?
- What are your fears concerning letting go of *all* your unfinished business? (List them.)
- Offer yourself the gift of love and gratitude for taking on this deep and healing work.

Higher Self-Talk

I feel a shift toward lightness and spaciousness. I feel the pains and stories of my past loosening their grip on me and freeing up space for all my future blessings. I know this is a process, and that there is more to be done and more to clear out. I know that just because I have identified the paths to letting go and written a letter to one person doesn't mean I'm done with this work; there may be more people who I am holding onto and more stories I have yet to unearth. I will allow my mind and heart to investigate further and to release whatever is necessary. I embrace the journey and accept that life is filled with challenges I now know how to recover from. I am hopeful, confident, and excited to move forward into total clarity and freedom. I have the tools I need to walk my path with joy and lightness. I know I am always just a pen and paper away from releasing what is holding me back. I am so grateful for all the blessings and lessons in my life and all the experiences that have brought me to this moment of total forgiveness, clarity, and freedom. I can now create anything my heart desires.

Chapter 14:
Lesson 7

Hi, it's Melanie and I am my own client. I want to share with you a part of my happier ending story and how I moved from tremendous loss and transition into a life custom-built for me. I promise, I wouldn't have spent this many years of my life working to get this process on paper if it hadn't already brought so much freedom, joy, and self-wisdom into my own life. I thought it might help to see the introduction of my fairy-tale story to get you started. Here it goes:

"Once upon a time there was a young child who was born into a world of chaos and uncertainty. There were many obstacles to overcome. Many dragons to be slain. Many heartbreaks to survive. Many fears to be conquered. This was not an easy quest—but she was not your typical child. The sorcerer chose her specifically for this journey. Here is the story and the mission of a warrior child whose destiny was to understand the deep wounding of her soul and the soul of others. Her path through the dark night was not in vain; it was a supremely crafted course built to bestow her with the knowledge and the courage to bring love and forgiveness into the mainstream of the world. She would not know she was on this journey until her heart

was healed and her spirit was strong. It was a journey that at times would bring her to her knees—but it also taught her the depth of her own brave heart and the vastness of her unencumbered soul. Through perseverance and faith, she was gifted with the vision of what was possible when one learned the art and the majesty of pure love and total forgiveness."

Have fun with this, and let your imagination soar!

....

"We cannot wish old feelings away nor do spiritual exercises for overcoming them until we have woven a healing story that transforms our previous life's experience and gives meaning to whatever pain we have endured."

–JOAN BORYSENKO

Wow! We are in the final stage of the work. Take a deep breath and a moment to absorb any changes you're feeling, and to congratulate yourself on your courage and hard work. Getting to know oneself at a deep level is a powerful thing. Taking a detailed look at where we came from, how we have performed in the world, the habits and patterns we have developed, and the choices we have made is, to say the least, eye-opening and emotional. This is okay. Let it be as it is. The charge will pass, and you will find more space and freedom as the days pass and you become more familiar with who you are now that you're clear of baggage, stories, and unfinished business.

For me, opening more and more to myself, my life, and my past was exciting—and kind of scary. I was thrilled to discover so much about why I was the way I was, and to know that I had found a way to heal and open myself to the future I was meant to live. But the knowledge that my life was solely in my hands—that the choices that I made and would make in the future were now truly *my* choices, up to me and only me, with no blame, no shame, no hiding—was frightening. Ultimately, though, the excitement won out. I knew that I had taken my power back and called my soul back home, and I could feel the vastness of my life and all the potential it held. My innate wisdom returned naturally, and I saw life and all its possibilities in a fresh new way.

Now it's time for you to get to the next phase of your life: the work of replanting your garden. Now that your soil is clean and clear, free of all those weeds and clutter, it's time to create and design.

This is where real choices, made from a neutral place, start to evolve. These choices are our seeds to nurture and grow into the life of our dreams—or, shall we say, the life of our *choice*!

In this final chapter, we will retell the story of our lives and plant a vision of what is possible when we operate from a new perspective—one that is bright, positive, and truly meaningful to our growth. Then we will solidify that story and move into creating our future vision from the future backward!

The Happier Ending

Let's start with the "happier ending" story of our life.

This next exercise is based on the premise that people who believe their lives to be meaningful tend to tell stories defined by growth, possibility, community, and self-efficacy. Using the art of *the story* to deliberately craft a positive identity and to reframe our past and self-image creates possibility and positivity and is a profound tool that has been shown to produce results. Stories about being loved, being in the driver's seat of our lives, and having the ability to take whatever obstacles we have encountered and turn them into good and useful outcomes has an enormous effect on future success.

In my years studying positive psychology, one of the most powerful tools I learned—what I consider to be one of the great contributions of modern psychology and its research—was that of editing, reframing, rewriting, and reinterpreting the stories we have been telling ourselves for a lifetime. Rewriting our stories from an intentionally positive perspective can help us feel and believe that we are in control of our life and the hardships we've encountered have only added strength and purpose to it. Studies have shown that even making small edits to our life story can have a huge impact on our performance and outcomes.

What might life look like if we viewed it from a different angle? For this lesson, we will go back to your shadow side events (the ones you wrote back in Lesson 5!) and rewrite them as a story with a fresh point of view—a "reframe," as positive psychology terms it. I call it the *recoding*!

Reframing our lives is a way of shining a new light on our experiences and allowing our brain to take a fresh snapshot of each one. This literally changes our point of view on any given situation. The facts may remain the same, but by making a deliberate shift in how we see it, new outcomes and possible futures are created.

Here, we are going to rewrite our shadow side events as fairy tales. Instead of my client Caroline's story of "I was never enough for my father because he always wanted another boy," she might reframe it as, "Once upon a time there was a little girl born to a man who needed a great lesson on how to love fully, without conditions or expectations. That little girl was a magical wizard who was chosen to take this life lesson on as purpose and to bring it into the world to help others see how to love unconditionally and to live their mission and purpose in life without judgment."

This is the writing of the happier ending. Remember, life will still have its twists and turns, so allow your creativity to include them. Go back and look at your shadow story, keeping an eye out for the potential and the positive. Look for the meaning, the lessons, and, just like in a fairy tale, the moral of the story. Spin everything into the positivity of possibility, even if it involves a challenge. See it from the lens of potential and meaning. It's not what happened *to* me, it's what happened *for* me, and how can I use that to build my greatest future. All the things that happened in your life are now seen not as detention but as "life school," with a curriculum designed specifically to support you becoming exactly who you were meant to be. You are writing a story of gratitude for what has happened and for what was gained—in other words, the "I see everything that is possible; I am the warrior, the co-creator, the hero of my own profoundly powerful story" version. This is you flipping the lens to the beautiful, bright, Technicolor version of your life. In this story you are the journeyman, the guide, the healer, and the hero. You are *never* the victim!

You don't have to get overly heavy in going back to thank certain relationships and situations for helping you grow. Here's an example: I had a very difficult relationship with one of my sisters. To reframe my experiences with her, I could say, "Thank you so much. I would have never become the warrior I am today if I hadn't had to survive all of the things you were in my life. You were my boot camp; you were my blessing. I can play big in the world because our relationship taught me to have the courage to stand up for myself. You made me bold, brave, and strong. I would have been so naïve if you hadn't taught me to honor myself and get clear on what is true and real in life. I wouldn't have the skill set I have now if I hadn't always had to be on my toes and stay calm in the face of challenges I needed to overcome. You were my greatest teacher. I am truly grateful for you."

You can have fun with this by turning it into a real "Once upon a time . . ." fairy tale, as I did at the start of this chapter, but if that doesn't feel authentic to you, you don't have to!

A note before we begin: If this looks like spiritual/emotional bypassing to you—it's not! Why? Because we do not do this *in lieu* of the work; we do this after already having done the work to clear out the clutter of the past as we used to perceive it. This part of the journey is only possible once we've tossed out all that old stuff and are ready for a clear view from an open window.

Lesson 7 Homework: Your Happier Ending

This week's homework can be playful and magical. Bring back the imaginative child in you. Become any character or superhero you desire. Don't let this story weigh you down (*retrenching*); let it lift you up and set you free. And don't forget to have fun!

✸ STEP 1: WRITING YOUR HAPPIER ENDING

Now it's time to revisit your shadow story and rewrite it to reflect your highest potential. This is your opportunity to dream and envision your life from a higher altitude—your time to embrace the big-picture *you*! Pay attention to the possibility of all things and see your story through the perspective of "life school" preparing you to become the most empowered version of yourself.

Please have fun with this exercise. Be as creative as you would like. Use colored pens or pictures or special paper. This is something you will want to keep and refer to from time to time. Remember that *recoding* your story in this way gives you the opportunity to be the author of your life—the designer and keeper of your garden. Make it a big, beautiful, audacious one!

✹ STEP 2: LIFE SCHOOL AND FLIPPING THE LENS

This work is forging new neural pathways. We've already organized and transferred out the old emotions associated with these experiences, permanently. Now we're switching perspectives and re-imprinting and recoding those experiences in your brain—in all three of your brains, in fact.

You have now learned, with absolute authenticity, a process that will help you to understand the trauma and grief of certain life experiences and know that you can choose and work toward an incredibly peaceful outcome. You now know how to consistently release unfinished business before getting bogged down by it. You won't choose to stay in discomfort or pain anymore; instead, you will acknowledge every trauma—big or small, chronic or acute; do the work it takes to release it; and choose to move on with your life. As you do this on an ongoing basis, it will become second nature.

Questions for reflection:

- What does it look like to establish relationships now that the old stories have been recoded?
- What does it look like to make different choices when the world around me appears the same?
- What practices can I adopt to assist me in moving forward when fresh awareness arises after completing this work?
- Are there people I already trust deeply with whom I can create a buddy system moving forward?

✺ STEP 3: REVERSE AND RE-CREATE

Now that we have completed our unfinished business of the past, reframed our story, and stepped into a clear and bright present, let's create the possibilities for a dynamic and masterful future!

One of the techniques I have always found to be powerfully effective is the use of reverse timelines. These are timelines that start us off in the biggest and brightest future version of ourselves and then move us backward to the now. Building our vision and our plans backward in this way helps us create far bigger changes in our lives.

Once we have a clear vision of our greatest tomorrow, it's crucial to check in and make sure it also works moving forward into the future from the present. This helps us to ground our vision. When we clearly see and feel the compelling future we desire, it helps us to access a better inner state. From that elevated inner state, we can find better inner resources, which will, in turn, assist us in creating better and more desirable plans.

In contrast, when we envision our plans moving from today forward, we tend to design more incrementally and end up with what's called "small chunk" plans. We also tend to be less daring and creative. One thing we don't want to forget is that the past, especially the challenging parts, holds tremendous data and resources that we can learn and grow from. Past data that informs our future is an asset. Positive memories feed the higher states that we want to access, now and in the future. Negative experiences give us tremendous lessons and tools that support our growth and development. They literally make us smarter—if we can perceive them correctly. Weeds can actually nourish a garden, making the topsoil more supportive and increasing its health, if the garden they grow in is being cared for properly. So don't just ignore their value. Honor them.

As you have learned in this book, when dealing with the more negative experiences of the past, it's essential to keep their most powerful and life-affirming lessons and blessings even as you discard the emotional baggage they've saddled you with. You are now an expert at impartially asking the question, "What have I gained from this experience or relationship, what can I carry forward into my brightest future, and what do I need to let go of and release fully?" Focusing on what is useful and supportive is the key to utilizing this gained wisdom of the past as a tool for growth.

This neurolinguistic programming (NLP) technique you are about to experience first came into use in the seventies and has had great impact on people's future outcomes. It reveals an inner timeline that, you'll find, you already use regularly in your daily life. It's a mirroring of a natural process we use to sort our days, weeks, months, and years. In visualizing your timeline, you're seeing what is, in theory, a hologram of something that's been inside of you ever since you grasped the concept of time—just like the acorn that already holds the vison, structure, and potential of the great oak it will grow to be.

Timeline Exercise #1: Visualization

There are many different timeline exercises out there. This one—simple, fun, and easy to complete—is an amalgam of the many I have used over the years:

> 1. *Take a comfortable seat.* Using your full imagination, imagine the future ahead of you as a full and expansive field, bursting with vibrant possibilities and promise. Next, envision your past as a field stretching out behind you. Take your time. Once you feel clarity of vision in both directions, take the

time to name and design your future desires and all the things you could do to manifest them.

2. Fully envision yourself and your life far into the future. Imagine that you've created the life that you truly want and that you are living it fully, three-dimensionally and in color. What does it look like? Specifically, what do you see, smell, hear? Deeply connect and experience the image you have created; take some time to enjoy the feeling of it.

3. Detach and dissociate. Take yourself outside of the frame and look at it all—present to future—as if it has already come to pass. From this bird's-eye view, list three key elements that helped you achieve this outcome.

4. Take yourself halfway back to present time. Notice all the things you did to implement or create those three key elements. Could you have done more? Could you improve on what you did?

5. Place yourself back in present time. What can you do, starting now, to begin the process of realizing those elements in your life today?

6. Envision yourself bringing those elements into your life. Really imagine yourself moving forward into the future. See yourself conquering any possible obstacles that might place themselves in your path. See yourself moving along on this journey, all the way to your intended goal—the outcome of your dreams.

7. *Listen to your future.* Does it have any wisdom to share with you? Standing in your empowered and successful future, what words of wisdom would your future-self have to share with you?

8. *Stand in the present.* Move into the "future you" and take in all the deep wisdom and knowing you have gained. Gift that same wisdom and knowing to your present self.

9. *Show gratitude to your present self.* Give thanks to yourself for showing the courage, and taking the time and energy, to envision the future self and life you hope to create.

Timeline Exercise #2: Neurolinguistic Programming
Imagine a line and see your future completely stretched out in front of you. Take your time. Really use your imagination. Visualization can be challenging for some but go slow and stay open. It's like meditation. It may not be easily at first but stay with it and it will change your life. Now, see your days, weeks, months, and years systematically arranged in order, one day after another. This is a model of your inner sense of time—your personal timeline. You will use it to plan, design, and schedule your journey. It's like holding a Google calendar in your mind.

First, you must commit to the idea that you will reach your envisioned goal or destination at some point in time— no matter what.

Next, you are going to visualize yourself moving forward on your timeline until you get to the place in your future where you have accomplished your goal / reached your desired destination.

Now review and make sure that everything happened in a way that you are satisfied with. If it didn't, take the time to change it until you are completely satisfied with your process.

Next, turn around and look back at your entire timeline, taking note of everything that occurred along the way to reaching your ultimate goal. What actions did you take to move yourself closer to accomplishing your goal? Hold that vision and record *exactly* what you did every step of the way.

Voilà! You have your road map to your desired future. You know how you will get to the future of your design.

To make this even more satisfying, take a good look at the map you've just created. Be aware of any detours or unnecessary stops you took along the way. Keep using the higher, overhead view of your timeline to refine every detail until your map is as clear and clean as you can get it. Continue to practice and master this exercise.

Finally, put your plan in writing. All that's left now is to follow through; it's time to project the magnificence of possibilities onto your path. Now that you have removed the past's hooks from your life and are holding the road map to your future, joy is a choice you are free to make—you are unstoppable!

Homework Follow-Up

You cannot live an abundant, joy-filled life if you are still identifying with the old, stale, unfinished business of the past. Dropping the weight of yesterday's disappointments and heartbreaks and choosing to vibrate at the speed of love will bring quantum changes to your life. It's true that you can't have light without dark or land without water. You also cannot have joy without sorrow or gratitude without grief. These dualities help us recognize our circumstances.

We are meant to learn and grow from these experiences, however—not live in them to our own detriment!

To get on with your life, you need to understand, forgive, and get to the other side—which is exactly what you've done over these last many weeks. Bravo for showing up for yourself, your heart, and your future!

Reflections:

- Think of how you can continue to clear old perspectives and release negative interpretations of the actions of others.
- Actively track the behavioral patterns in your relationships with others; notice the ones that recur most often.
- As you go forward, continue this practice: release old relationships and unfinished business and take inventory of attitudes and beliefs that disempower you or make you feel victimized so you don't reestablish them and carry them with you into the future.
- Take note of beliefs that you still automatically accept or react to emotionally, even though you know they are not true.
- Are there events or relationships from the past about which you still feel judgmental? Check with your three brains on this one.
- List all your excuses for hanging on to the past, if there are any left. (Look hard—they can be sneaky!)
- What deep insights have occurred for you during this work? Take note of them in your workbook or journal.
- Is there anything—any person, any event—that still intimidates you or brings up guilt, anger, shame, jealousy, or fear in you?

- Are there any remaining stories or beliefs you hold that you would like to examine, change, and rewrite? Are you willing to change them?
- Are you willing and able to start viewing your life from a more impersonal perspective—willing to take a thirty-thousand-foot view that allows for greater objectivity and possibility?
- List the changes the world would see in you—and you would experience for yourself—if you fully embraced an objective and conscious view of your life and the choices you now make from a clear and completed past.
- Do you feel any fear around making any changes you have committed to during this work?
- Write an incantation that reminds you each day that you are standing in your power and fully designing your life from a place of passion, joy, and inner truth!

Higher Self-Talk

I honor myself and the commitment I've made to own my journey. I take my power back. I call my soul back home. My body and energy systems feel clear and clean. I am so grateful to have had the courage and the wisdom to let go of all that no longer serves me and to empower my mind, body, and soul. Although I may never know why certain events occur in my life, I now have the self-respect and inner trust to know that I can manage anything, forgive anything, and create anything. I have the tools to make the choices needed to keep myself emotionally and energetically healthy. Now that I know how to take full responsibility for my actions, reactions, and choices, my future is in my control.

I will continue to keep watch over myself and do the work it takes to live a fully loving and empowered life. I will give from a place of honest and open vulnerability, without fear or blocks. I will no longer take life's twists and turns personally. I will no longer lose my power to people or occurrences that are not mine to carry—not now or ever again. I am committed to leaving the past behind, striving for self-awareness, and accepting nothing less than what I have been put on this earth to manifest. I am wholly myself. My heart is full. My soul is free.

Chapter 15:

Conclusion

How do you feel? Notice any changes, big or small. When we thresh our past, we are left with open spaces that may feel odd or even haunting. Let them be. Give them time. The universe does not allow a vacuum to exist for long, and it will fill in that space for you when it's right. However, you must stand guard. Lovingly block the entry of anything or anyone that may feel negative or push you back into repeating and regrooving old patterns. Keep the relationships you've just cleared out clean and full of awareness. Do not fall into or retrench old habits. Recode the new, liberated, and open you! It's a wonderful thing to finish up our unfinished business, create a deeper connection with ourselves, and begin to see the bright promise of an unmarred future.

Some of you may wonder how to continue this work going forward. My clients have used this work for years, even long after our one-on-one or group work work was completed. I still do this work today and welcome new clients, but you are also welcome and encouraged to work with a friend or a group of friends. If you choose to do this work in community, please remember there is no judgment allowed, and opinions or comparisons are never a part of the process. You are there to be an open heart with curious, loving, compassionate ears—no more, no less.

Another wonderful addition to this work is any form of meditation or stillness practices, as well as prayers, blessings, and gratitude work. You can also journal or start a diary (watch out for the four Rs if you do! No naval-gazing or self-pity, please!), or add storyboarding to the menu. These are all perfect companions and travel buddies for this work. And please feel free to find or create your own.

This work is a deeply personal and intimate journey. Feel free to create and express; trust in your instincts, and give yourself the freedom to follow your intuition. Let your wisdom guide you!

Above all, please continue to do the work, now and forever. Living a powerful, magnificent life is a never-ending journey.

Take some time now and each day moving forward to reflect on the following journaling prompts.

- Each day, honor yourself for the insights you have gained and the guidance you have received during any of your meditations or prayers, or in the course of doing the personal growth work you continue to practice.
- Take inventory of the balance between the complaining versus the gratitude you voice (internally or to others) in your life. Do you need to recalibrate?
- Practice asking for guidance instead of for *things*. Notice your tendencies around this as you move through your days.
- Start each morning with the simplest prayer of all: "Thank you for my perfect life." Use it as a mantra whenever you meet challenges. You will be surprised by the immediate (positive) outcome.

- Have you cultivated a personal relationship with a higher energy—purpose, community, a higher power—free of any religious structure or rules? Do you feel you could refine that relationship further?
- Do you carry any expectations that the God of your own understanding will give you answers or explanations around any of the pain or loss you have experienced in your life? Does this seem reasonable to you? Can you seek instead to find a sense of gratitude in everything that comes into and out of your life?
- Take time to get clear on any instances in which you feel you have been duped, short-changed, or deserted because of some loss, trauma, or unfinished business that caused you suffering.
- Can you commit to doing the work around the issues that have surfaced in your mind and heart as we've moved through this process together?
- What might happen if you never found meaning for the heartbreak or grief in your life? How would that make you feel? How can you continue to infuse meaning into everything you do?
- Do you understand that there is always meaning in life, even when you don't get all the answers you desire?
- Can you commit some time each day to being fully aware of the blessings and gifts each one of us has?
- How willing are you to practice meditation, prayer, and gratitude each day for five or ten or twenty minutes, once or twice a day, knowing it will bring more peace and healing to your soul and life?
- Are you committed to continuing to do this work around loss, trauma, and any other unfinished business that may come up for you in the future?

- Remind yourself every day to *love yourself, and to always choose healing over hurting.*

We have come to the end of this journey together. I cannot thank you enough for putting your time, effort, and faith into this work. You will continue to feel the effects of this process for months and years to come. I have been doing this work on myself for over two decades now, and in that time my life has remained clear and open to all of life's possibilities—all opportunities to grow, change, and love. I often joke about the fact that even if I lose a nail, I do my UFB work. I can tell you firsthand, if you continue to do this work, clearing every event (small, medium, or large) that merits attention from your mind, body, and soul, you will create a life filled with joy, peace, clarity, and prosperity— a garden lush with magnificent blooms and free from the weeds of shame, fear, and unfinished business. Put simply, you will become the happiest, most loving person you know.

May you live your highest, most profoundly beautiful life. May you carry with you the wisdom and clarity required to navigate life's challenges and call your spirit and power back home. May the accumulation of unfinished business be a thing of your past. May you move forward in your life knowing that no matter what the future holds, you will remain rooted, grounded, and empowered in the clean and nourished garden of your soul.

Carry on, you beautiful gardeners and soldiers of the highest good!

The light within me salutes the light within you. Now and forever.

NAMASTE,

MELANIE

Appendix 1:

Holmes and Rahe Stress Scale

There are so many events that can count as heartbreaks, losses, traumas, and stressors that in 1967 psychiatrists Holmes and Rahe examined the medical records of over five thousand medical patients to determine whether stressful events might cause illnesses. Patients were asked to tally a list of forty-three life events based on a relative score. A direct correlation was found between their life events and their illnesses.

When I look at their list, I see heartbreak—I see trauma. I also see that they are missing quite a few biggies, like betrayal by a loved one, friend, or lover; abuse or sexual assault; change in sexual identity; and many others. Please feel free to add these, or anything else that you feel defines your event more accurately than the top twelve I provided in Chapter 10, or the ones listed below. But also see if your more specific definition can fit into the top twelve that I provided earlier; for example, loss of memory is more specific, but could also fall under the umbrella of "loss of control of your body."

Again, if you do not consider your UFB event to be represented in the top twelve, please refer to this list or you can follow your intuition and name it yourself. Your ultimate goal is to put your events into twelve categories.

According to the Holmes and Rahe Stress Scale, an individual's stress can be measured by adding together the number of "Life Change Units" that apply to events in the past year of that person's life.

If you want to tally your level of stress, circle each event in this list that applies to you, and then calculate the final total by adding together the values assigned to each event:

Life Event / Life Change Units for Adults:

- Death of a spouse – 100
- Divorce – 73
- Marital separation – 65
- Imprisonment – 63
- Death of a close family member – 63
- Personal injury or illness – 53
- Marriage – 50
- Dismissal from work – 47
- Marital reconciliation – 45
- Retirement – 45
- Change in health of family member – 44
- Pregnancy – 40
- Sexual difficulties – 39
- Gain a new family member – 39
- Business readjustment – 39
- Change in financial state – 38
- Death of a close friend – 37
- Change to different line of work – 36
- Change in frequency of arguments – 35
- Major mortgage – 32
- Foreclosure of mortgage or loan – 30
- Change in responsibilities at work – 29

- Child leaving home – 29
- Trouble with in-laws – 29
- Outstanding personal achievement – 28
- Spouse starts or stops work – 26
- Beginning or ending school – 26
- Change in living conditions – 25
- Revision of personal habits – 24
- Trouble with boss – 23
- Change in working hours or conditions – 20
- Change in residence – 20
- Change in schools – 20
- Change in recreation – 19
- Change in church activities – 19
- Change in social activities – 18
- Minor mortgage or loan – 17
- Change in sleeping habits – 16
- Change in number of family reunions – 15
- Change in eating habits – 15
- Vacation – 13
- Major holiday – 12
- Minor violation of law – 11

Total

Total Score of 300+: At risk of illness.
Score of 150–299: Risk of illness is moderate (reduced by 30 percent from the above risk).
Score <150: Only have a slight risk of illness.

Life Event / Life Change Units for Non-adults

- Death of parent – 100
- Unplanned pregnancy/abortion – 100
- Getting married – 95
- Divorce of parents – 90

- Acquiring a visible deformity – 80
- Fathering a child – 70
- Jail sentence of parent for over one year – 70
- Marital separation of parents – 69
- Death of a brother or sister – 68
- Change in acceptance by peers – 67
- Unplanned pregnancy of sister – 64
- Discovery of being an adopted child – 63
- Marriage of parent to stepparent – 63
- Death of a close friend – 63
- Having a visible congenital deformity – 62
- Serious illness requiring hospitalization – 58
- Failure of a grade in school – 56
- Not making an extracurricular activity – 55
- Hospitalization of a parent – 55
- Jail sentence of parent for over thirty days – 53
- Breaking up with boyfriend or girlfriend – 53
- Beginning to date – 51
- Suspension from school – 50
- Becoming involved with drugs or alcohol – 50
- Birth of a brother or sister – 50
- Increase in arguments between parents – 47
- Loss of job by parent – 46
- Outstanding personal achievement – 46
- Change in parent's financial status – 45
- Accepted at college of choice – 43
- Being a senior in high school – 42
- Hospitalization of a sibling – 41
- Increased absence of parent from home – 38
- Brother or sister leaving home – 37
- Addition of third adult to family – 34
- Becoming a full-fledged member of a church – 31
- Decrease in arguments between parents – 27

- Decrease in arguments with parents – 26
- Mother or father beginning work – 26

Total

Total Score of 300+: At risk of illness.

Score of 150–299: Risk of illness is moderate (reduced by 30 percent from the above risk).

Score <150: Slight risk of illness.

Appendix 2:
Stress Indicators Continued

For the purpose of chart work only: here is a list of some stress indicators that may have started showing up in your life after you experienced trauma, loss, or heartbreak.

- You eat standing up.
- Your dog doesn't recognize you.
- You're always late.
- You forget what day it is.
- You have trouble finishing a sentence.
- Your friends greet you, "Hey, stranger!"
- You're drinking more than usual.
- You're fighting more than usual.
- You can't remember what "usual" is.
- You do three things at once; you don't finish any of them.
- You lose your keys. And your glasses. And your patience.
- You only talk to people via email/text.
- You're always tired.
- You can't sleep.
- You keep getting sick.

- You keep dropping things.
- You bite your nails, tap your feet, and twirl your hair. All at the same time.
- You feel like you're drowning.
- You don't have time to feed your fish.
- Your blood pressure is too high.
- Your morale is too low.
- You jump when the phone rings.
- You eat. And eat. And eat.
- You have a headache. Again.
- Your palms are sweaty.
- Your heart is racing.
- You feel nervous or jumpy.
- Nothing seems fun anymore.
- You snap at your friends.
- Your socks don't match.
- You yell at your partner.
- You hate getting up in the morning.
- You drive too fast.
- You talk too fast.
- You cry at the drop of a hat.
- You can't breathe.
- You can't concentrate.
- You keep bumping into things.
- You can't see over the laundry.
- You're never alone.
- You're always alone.
- You live on coffee, cigarettes, or diet soda.
- You haven't opened mail in days.
- It's always someone else's fault
- People keep asking, "Are you okay?"
- You wonder if you are okay.

There are many more, so feel free to add some of your own!

Appendix 3: Identifying *Your* Heartbreak Category and Type

Look at your life through a microscope and think back to the major losses, changes, and transitions you've experienced. List your top three to five. Were they acute or chronic? Which loss bucket does your event fall into (e.g. "loss of control of body," "loss of trust," etc.)?

LOSS MEMORY	ACUTE OR CHRONIC	TYPE OF LOSS
EXAMPLE: Loss of my father at age 15. **EXAMPLE:** Dad tells you you're "stupid" daily	Acute and chronic	Loss of dreams, Loss of a loved one Loss of self, Loss of trust, Loss of dignity etc.
1.		
2.		
3.		
4.		
5.		

Appendix 4:
Terms Overview

AACTS (ACCEPTANCE AND APPROVAL CREATE TRICKS): The false face or actions one adopts—the coping behaviors one acquires—so they can appear to be in control, and ensure that they feel or are accepted by individuals or groups.

BLAME: Assigning responsibility to others for a fault or wrong. Case-building against another to protect yourself.

CHARGE: The energetic interface between mind and body. This is your life force, your energetic circuitry, the magic of being alive. Bioenergetic therapy calls this energy charge. We define blocked charge as stored, frozen, and incomplete energy that is held in the body and must be released and completed. Blocked charge is the protective response to significant heartbreaks, traumas, losses, feelings, and ideas that we hold in, hold back, and hold onto. These feelings do not vaporize; rather, they live within the body until completed.

CHARGE CHANGERS: Activities, distractions, or actions taken in order to change or avoid the uncomfortable and often painful feelings caused by heartbreaking or high-impact experiences. These activities are used to shift the charge in the body to abate our discomfort, and when they stop the completion of stored or blocked charge, they trap that energy in the body. This keeps our feelings hidden and buried until a trigger comes along, making us repeat our learned avoidance and coping behaviors.

OVERCHARGED: When your body kicks into overdrive, typically activated by a trigger. This can show up as anxiety, anger, hyper-alertness, nervousness, ADD, a need for attention, or acts of aggression. It can show up in an instant with hot thoughts or an impulse to react, almost not knowing what hit you.

UNDERCHARGED: This is a drop in energy and can be subtle or severe. Perhaps you feel tired, lethargic, lazy, and have the need to zone out. Maybe you can't make clear decisions or focus, and you have a hard time getting motivated. Being undercharged can also show up as depression.

DESTINED LIFE: A life of choice, wisdom, design, and action. A life where you see things as they "are," and not the way you "wish" they were. A life where you deliberately move toward a desired outcome.

FATED LIFE: A resistance to a new way of being, thinking, and proceeding. A life that lacks deliberate choices and action. A victimized perspective of life that pushes forward the belief that you have no control over what happens to or for you.

GUILT: "I did something wrong."

SHAME: "I am something wrong."

HEARTBREAK: The reality that something is gone, over, changed, irretrievable, or irreversible. The feeling of overwhelming distress that needs to be dealt with in order to fully heal and move on with our lives. Heartbreaks come in many forms; it changes the natural flow of our energy and will ultimately impact, typically in a negative way, our reaction to and ability to function within the world.

LOSS: The process of losing something or someone, or a consistent pattern of behavior and way of being. Being deprived of something of significance. A profound event that leaves you feeling stressed, depleted, heartbroken, or out of control, leading to discordance of emotions and thoughts.

MODELS AND MANTRAS: Spoken and unspoken patterns and beliefs that have been learned, acquired, and adopted from our early environment. We take on these ways of being as our truth, beliefs, and habits because it's all we know and have witnessed in our developmental years. They are the inner rules that govern our behaviors, choices, and beliefs.

FAMILY OF ORIGIN: The people who initiated your patterns and helped shape who you have become.

REFLECTING: The act of reviewing the story of your life, or pieces of it, without judgment or embellishment in order to understand, organize, and find the clarity needed to move forward, heal, and let go.

REMINISCING: The act of remembering and contemplating your past from a romantic, embellished, and charged place.

RUMINATING: The act of thinking about the same thing over and over, on a loop, and in doing so becoming stuck and unable to move forward.

RETRENCHING: The act of reliving our past repeatedly, thereby feeding into its negative energy and digging deeper pathways in the brain around each event and their associated memories.

SOMATIC HEALING: A form of body-centered therapies that looks at the connection between mind and body and uses both psychotherapy and physical therapies for holistic healing.

ACUTE EVENT: Sudden losses, demands, and pressures that impact or traumatize us in the moment and can create present and future damage.

CHRONIC EVENTS: Long-term, consistent behaviors, losses, demands, and pressures that erode us over time and shape the way we see and function in the world.

TRAUMA: Our understanding of trauma—what it is and how to define it—is ever-evolving. At its most basic, it can be understood as the emotional response that results from experiencing a distressing or life-altering event that damages a person's sense of safety and self, as well as their ability to regulate their emotions and establish healthy relationships. On a more complex level, it can be understood as the "gradual constriction of freedom" and "undermining of our self-esteem, self-confidence, feelings of well-being, and connection to life" (Levine) or as something that causes you to "organize your life as if the trauma were still going on—unchanged and immutable—as every new encounter or event is contaminated by the past" (van der Kolk). It's vital to remember that trauma is not defined by the size or nature of the event but instead by what happens inside of us as a result of that event. Trauma is what lives inside a person, not the event itself; it is not the story of what occurred but rather the pain and terror that event imprinted upon the person who lived it.

Endnotes

1. Bessel van der Kolk, *The Body Keeps the Score: Brain, Mind, and Body in the Healing of Trauma* (New York: Penguin Books, 2015), 235.

2. Merriam-Webster 2023, s.v. "soul," https://www.merriam -webster.com/dictionary/soul#citations.

3. "The Law of Reflection," The Physics Classroom, accessed January 24, 2023, https://www.physicsclassroom. com/class/refln/Lesson-1/The-Law-of-Reflection.

4. "The Three Brains: Why Your Head, Heart and Gut Sometimes Conflict," Australian Spinal Research Foundation, July 26, 2016, https://spinalresearch.com.au/three-brains -head-heart-gut-sometimes-conflict.

5. Van der Kolk, 208.

6. Donna Jackson Nakazawa, *Childhood Disrupted: How Your Biography Becomes Your Biology, and How You Can Heal* (New York: Atria Books, 2015).

7. James W. Pennebaker, PhD, and John F. Evans, EdD, *Expressive Writing: Words That Heal* (Enumclaw, WA: Idyll Arbor, 2014), 3.

8. Pennebaker and Evans, 19.

9. Wikipedia, s.v. "Persona (psychology)," last modified April 16, 2022, 20:34, https://en.wikipedia.org/wiki/Persona _(psychology).

10. Carl G. Jung, *Memories, Dreams, Reflections* (New York: Vintage Books, 1989), 356.

11. Mayukh Saha, "14 Enlightening Quotes from Carl Jung to Delve Deep into Your Psyche," last modified February 6, 2020, https://truththeory.com/14-enlightening-quotes -from-carl-jung-to-delve-deep-into-your-psyche.

12. Jessie Sholl, "How to Deal with Shame," last modified June 7, 2019, https://experiencelife.lifetime.life/article/shutting -shame-down.

13. Rachel Nichols, "Peter Levine on Somatic Experiencing: A Mind-Body Approach to Healing," last modified February 27, 2019, http://www.sfyogamagazine.com/ blog/2018/6/3/1r73uradcmg3k6eneiw377trwxgvoy#.

14. Anodea Judith, *Charge and the Energy Body: The Vital Key to Healing Your Life, Your Chakras, and Your Relationship* (New York: Hay House, 2018), 14.

15. Alexander Lowen, MD, *The Voice of the Body: The Role of the Body in Psychotherapy* (Burlington, Vermont: The Alexander Lowen Foundation, 2005).

16. Peter A. Levine, *Healing Trauma: A Pioneering Program for Restoring the Wisdom of Your Body* (Boulder, CO: Sounds True, 2008), 16.

17. Lindsey Tanner, "How Severe, Ongoing Stress Can Affect a Child's Brain," last modified July 12, 2017, https://www.nbclosangeles.com/news/national-international/toxic-stress-children-study-health/2028582.

18. Nadine Burke Harris, *The Deepest Well: Healing the Long-Term Effects of Childhood Adversity* (New York: Houghton Mifflin Harcourt, 2018), 58.

19. Stuart Wolpert, "That Giant Tarantula Is Terrifying, but I'll Touch It," last modified September 4, 2012, https://www.uclahealth.org/news/that-giant-tarantula-is-terrifying-but-ill-touch-it.

20. Wolpert.

21. Henry Fountain, "Let Us Give Thanks. In Writing," last modified November 22, 2007, https://www.nytimes.com/2007/11/22/fashion/22grateful.html.

22. Margarita Tartakovksy, MS, "The Power of Writing: 3 Types of Therapeutic Writing," last modified January 19, 2015, https://psychcentral.com/blog/the-power-of-writing-3-types-of-therapeutic-writing#1.

Acknowledgments

I have always believed that life is divinely on track. So much so that I consistently told my son when he was a child, "You may always ask G-d questions, but you may never question G-d." The Divine got it right. However, we tend to forget that this life is a curriculum. It is designed specifically for us, and what we learn from it is entirely up to us. What can diminish us and our experience of life is a refusal to learn, to accept and find meaning in both the ups and the downs of our personal journey. Our resistance to change and our unwillingness to surrender to a universal wisdom greater than our own personal knowing can be the antagonist of our own story. The one that takes us down. The one that makes us smaller than we are designed to be.

Learn to let go and you'll grow. Period. The work I've shared in this book has changed the way and the ease in which I let go of things. It has given me the one gift I believe we all long for: freedom.

The people I am about to thank are all on some level a fiber, a strand, or a stroke of color, texture, and meaning in the content you have engaged in over the last weeks. They are the ones who have healed me, grown with me, loved me, and believed in me and all I stand for in this life. I am humbled and blessed to call each of them both friend and angel. They are a part of each waking moment of my life. Like a river that collects pieces of everything it flows past, I carry them with me. Without the people who follow, I would be nothing but thin, thin air; in fact, I would be nothing at all.

Here it goes.

....

First, I would like to thank my son, Gideon, who is my heart, my soul, and my main purpose for being a human on this planet at this time. You have, solely through your existence, created more meaning and enthusiasm for me in this life than I ever thought possible. Your humor, love, and depth have grown my heart and vision infinitely. You have healed the broken spaces and encouraged my growth and stretch without even knowing it. Or did you? I love you beyond words, and I am grateful for you each day. I carry your heart. I carry it in my heart.

Next, I would like to thank my best friend and partner, Burt. Your ability to love everything about me (well?), and to see me so clearly, is a gift most people do not have the privilege of experiencing so deeply in a partnership. Your humor, kindness, humility, and patience make my life a joy. Thank you for letting me spend eight hours a day for the past two years or more getting my work and my passion on paper. You are such a goodie and I love you so very much.

Mary Currant Hackett. What can I say? Your encouragement and belief in my ability to write has been immeasurable. Your genius, wisdom, and honesty kept me going and made all the difference in the completion of this work. Thank you for forcing me not to use a ghostwriter and to trust my own voice, my own cadence, and my ability to get the truth of my journey in black and white. You were so right.

No one else could have done it and I would have been very disappointed in myself for copping out. As a friend, you are pure pedigree. I could not have done this without you, nor would I have wanted to.

Kimberly Petticolas. Thank you for the edits, the organization, the straight talk, and for acting as my sounding board. You are dynamite.

Everyone at She Writes Press—Brooke Warner, Lauren Wise, Elke Barter, Tabitha Lahr, and the amazing Krissa Lagos. Thank you for believing in me and my work and for the primping and polishing to get it pub-ready. And thank you for walking this newbie through it all. Your knowledge is stellar. I am so proud of what we've created together! Now let's heal some hearts and change some lives.

To Crystal Patriarche, Tabitha Bailey, Leilani Fitzpatrick, and my team at BookSparks: thank you for taking me to market and teaching me how to navigate these waters!

David Guc—my agent, manager, and BFF, and the male me—thank you for believing in me for the past 110 years. Even through the roughest waters. You're right, I am "the girl who figures it out"!

Chris Gaskill, my little brother and web-dude! I would be invisible without you.

Michael Galyon, thank you for the beauty.

Sara Allen, thank you for your intelligence, your heart, your courage and for being the wizard behind the curtain at the start of it all. I may never have started this journey without your support, patience and never-ending humor.

....

To my teachers:

We are set on our paths by our teachers and mentors, whether we know it or not. It is, however, up to each of us to choose how we use that wisdom to create our lives and purpose, as well as how we help the world around us with it. I have been blessed with some of the greatest of both.

Thank you beyond measure to Anodea Judith, my most treasured teacher, friend, and mentor. You led me down a path of self-understanding many years ago, and I am still walking it today. Your depth of knowledge of the body's energy system is vast and life-changing.

To Bessel van der Kolk: Thank you for helping me understand how the smaller events of our lives can be the things that shake our world and crack our foundation. My studies with you so deepened my curiosity around trauma, healing, and a life of mindfulness. You also curbed my puppylike eagerness to heal the world with your simple but wise words as we left a noisy dining hall after I'd exhausted your ears with question after question: "Melanie, we cannot save them all, but it is possible to take them a great distance." I, to this day, have never met anyone with more knowledge or impact on the subjects of trauma and healing. You're a true genius.

To Tal Ben-Shahar. Your kindness and accessibility make you a truly unique teacher. You so authentically live what you teach, and that is what all leaders should be made of. Thank you so much for believing in me and my work and for teaching me the art of happiness.

Dr. Peter Levine: Finding you and your work was like finding the holy grail. The answer to healing. That's what I have to say about that!

Seth Godin, Bill Aulet, Mandy Aftel, Jim Curtan, Carolyn Myss, and Brené Brown: Layer upon layer, you deepened my knowledge in so many areas and allowed me to carry that wisdom forward.

Deb Brosan and Mark Megerman: My Gestalt journey began with you, and my growth as a coach was deeply impacted by your knowledge, patience, humor, and support.

Maty Ezraty: Thank you for the years of yoga, guidance, friendship, and laughter. You are missed daily by me and all the students whose lives you changed.

Mrs. Butterly, Miss Riggi, and Mrs. Musti—you started it all.

....

To my friends:

To thank you all in detail I would need to write an entirely separate book. Who would we be without the reflection of ourselves in the eyes and soul of another? To the following, I thank you for allowing me to see myself, my potential, my heart, and my purpose. Your reflection has been the road map. Who would I be if you hadn't tolerated my musings, laughed at my jokes, and held space for my tears? You championed me through the rapids and celebrated with me at every destination. You grew me up, helped me up, and pushed me forward. Though some of you are no longer in my life—simply because, well, that's life—you remain sisters (and a few brothers).

From the beginning: Lisa Isaacs, Jill Rosenfeld, Nancy Swartz, Mary Grace Lipski, Ma (Gracie) and Pa (Bobert) Lipski, and baby bro Bobby Lipski. Margo Kornfeld, Cori Feldman, Toby Block, Georgina O'Farrell, Kris and Jerry Becker, DeDe and Gordon McMahon, Mary Ellen Stuart (the yin to my yang), Valley Chamberlain, Susan Brown, John Pena, Terry Woods, Toni Alperin, Nancy McKeon (my ride or die BFF and sister from another mother), Cindy Crawford, Heidi Brooks, Nicole Horton, Jenny Belushi, Ryan Haddon, Jillian Neal, Jeannine Braden, Abby Kohl, Geoff and Sam Rose, Lauren and Mark Kahn, Mariel Freeman, Leanne Jacobs, Porter Carroll Jr., Wayne Warnecke; and Vaneese Thomas, Kevin Sullivan, and Eric Yavebaum. My producer Sirintip Phasuk—teacher, friend, daughter, co-creator, maestro, and one of a kind! Thank you all for patchworking my heart and soul together.

....

To my family:

To Roseann. My sister. My doppelganger. My first tragedy. The entrance to this journey of healing I have been on for over thirty years. The day we lost you was the hardest day of our lives. Losing you may have been the greatest teacher of all. Not a day goes by that I don't wonder who we would be today. As sisters. As friends. As twins.

To Simon and Tia, my big bro and my sister-mom. I love you both and you are my touchstones.

Shia, the oldest. I love you. I miss your whistle and I wish I'd gotten to know you better.

Ger, the next in line, I love you and I wish you only love and happiness.

To Monroe and Margie. You were wonderful parents. Mom, I lost you too young, and Pops, I lost you too soon. I had so many more questions. Thank you for calling out and supporting my courage and determination. For respecting my dreams and for never once telling me I couldn't do it. I love you both so very much and I feel blessed for the parts of you I carry with me everywhere I go. You have both given me the morals of a general and the heart of a servant. I offer my reverence and gratitude. I miss you every day.

To Mama Sue Goldstein and Poppa Bud Rubel: Thank you for all the love you have given me and for making sure I never became an orphan even after I became an orphan. You and yours gave me and Gideon a loving place in this world. You always provided a soft place to land and a perfect place to laugh—home sweet home, and never to be forgotten.

....

Lastly, I thank all of those who have broken my heart, and even some of my dreams, but never my will. I thank you most passionately, for you made me who I am today: a strong, compassionate, curious, relentless, and unstoppable warrior of a life well lived, well healed, and in alignment with a greater good. To all of you, I bow, for you created the cracks that let the light in. You are the luthiers that tuned this broken-open heart. The alchemists that purified this soul and turned it into radiant gold. To you I owe the most. To you I owe it all.

And to each and every one of you—my readers and fellow journeyers—I offer a heart filled with gratitude, love, and an unerring sense of humor about it all.

About the Author

MELANIE SMITH has worked in the field of heartbreak, grief, trauma, transition, loss, change, reinvention, and all things Unfinished Business for over two decades and has helped thousands of people change their lives profoundly. She started her career as a platinum-selling international songwriter and award-winning actress, starring and co-starring in shows such as: *As the World Turns, Melrose Place, Seinfeld, Curb Your Enthusiasm, Deep Space Nine*, and *The Division*, to name a few. As an entrepreneur, her award-winning lifestyle, wellness, and yoga center was considered to be one of the most well-respected in the country by sources such as *Vogue, Yoga Journal, Philadelphia Magazine*, and others. Now a powerful motivational speaker, writer, and leader,

Melanie has been a contributing writer for many national health and wellness magazines and holds the distinction of being an PCC-level ICF certified coach and an ICI-master-level coach. She is the proud mother of one grown son, Gideon. Born and raised in Scranton, Pennsylvania, she presently splits her time between New Hope, Pennsylvania, and Naples, Florida.

Author photo © Tess Steinkolk

SELECTED TITLES FROM SHE WRITES PRESS

She Writes Press is an independent publishing
company founded to serve women writers everywhere.
Visit us at www.shewritespress.com.

Painting Life: My Creative Journey Through Trauma by Carol K. Walsh. $16.95, 978-1-63152-099-0. Carol Walsh was a psychotherapist working with traumatized clients when she encountered her own traumatic experience; this is the story of how she used creativity and artistic expression to heal, recreate her life, and ultimately thrive.

Your Turn: Ways to Celebrate Life Through Storytelling by Dr. Tyra Manning. Operating from the premise that writing about life experiences offers a new perspective that can aid in healing old traumas and wounds and in celebrating the joys of fond memories, this inspirational workbook encourages and supports readers in exploring their experiences and feelings on the page.

Indestructible: The Hidden Gifts of Trauma by Krista Nerestant. $16.95, 978-1-63152-799-9. Krista Nerestant endured multiple traumas as a child in the Philippines and a young immigrant in the United States—yet she rose to face every obstacle she encountered with courage and self-love. Along the way, she found success and healing, discovered the hidden gifts of trauma, and eventually became a spiritual medium and inspirational leader in her community.

Negatively Ever After: A Skeptic's Guide to Finding Happiness by Deanna K. Willmon. $16.95, 978-1-63152-312-0. From achieving self-adoration and learning what gratitude truly means to determining whether sharing happiness is really a good idea, this realistic and accessible guide will help you harness your negativity and find your own inner happiness.

Stop Giving it Away: How to Stop Self-Sacrificing and Start Claiming Your Space, Power, and Happiness by Cherilynn Veland. $16.95, 978-1-63152-958-0. An empowering guide designed to help women break free from the trappings of the needs, wants, and whims of other people—and the self-imposed limitations that are keeping them from happiness.